Life's Too Short
to Miss the Big Picture

for Moms

Life's Too Short
to Miss the Big Picture

for Moms

MELANIE SIMPSON

LEAFWOOD
PUBLISHERS

LIFE'S TOO SHORT TO MISS THE BIG PICTURE (FOR MOMS)

LEAFWOOD
PUBLISHERS

Copyright 2012 by Melanie Simpson

ISBN 978-0-89112-105-3
LCCN 2011051953

Printed in the United States of America

Scripture quotations, unless otherwise noted, are from The Holy Bible, New International Version. Copyright 1984, International Bible Society. Used by permission of Zondervan Publishers.

Scripture quotations taken from The Message copyright 1993, 1994, 1995, 1996, 2000, 2001, 2002. Used by permission of NavPress Publishing Group.

Scripture quotations noted NLT are taken from the Holy Bible, New Living Translation, copyright 1996, 2004. Used by permission of Tyndale House Publishers, Inc., Wheaton, Illinois 60189. All rights reserved.

Scripture noted ASV is taken from the American Standard Version. All rights reserved.

Scripture quotations taken from the New American Standard Bible®, NASB, Copyright © 1960, 1962, 1963, 1968, 1971, 1972, 1973, 1975, 1977, 1995 by The Lockman Foundation. Used by permission. ("http://www.Lockman.org" www.Lockman.org)

LIBRARY OF CONGRESS CATALOGING-IN-PUBLICATION DATA
Simpson, Melanie, 1973-
 Life's too short to miss the big picture (for moms) / by Melanie Simpson.
  p. cm.
 ISBN 978-0-89112-105-3
 1. Mothers--Religious life. 2. Motherhood--Religious aspects--Christianity. I. Title.
 BV4529.18.S56 2012
 248.8'431--dc23

                                                                    2011051953

Cover design by Marc Whitaker
Interior text design by Sandy Armstrong

Leafwood Publishers is an imprint of
Abilene Christian University Press
1626 Campus Court
Abilene, Texas 79601

1-877-816-4455
www.leafwoodpublishers.com

12 13 14 15 16 17 / 7 6 5 4 3 2 1

Dedication

I dedicate this book to my own mother—

Thank you for all of the balanced meals you cooked, the long PTA meetings you endured to see me sing for ten minutes, the beautiful prom dress that you sewed even when you didn't have input on my date, and for the patience and love you showed in not putting me out on the curb during my teenage years.

Even when you did not know it, your loving, sacrificial heart was teaching mine how to love. And ultimately, love is the big picture.

Contents

Acknowledgments

Special thanks to my daddy for being a beautiful definition of "father" and my biggest fan.

Thanks to my husband, Michael, my partner in life, my inspiration, and my hero. Thank you for believing in my potential even when I occasionally struggle to see it in myself. You make me a better person and a better mom.

Finally, thanks to my children, Julia and Zeke, my unique and precious gifts from God. No matter what I achieve in life, you will always be my magnum opus.

All of you have given me a glimpse of the big picture.

Foreword

Throughout the centuries, no relationship has been more celebrated in art, literature, and culture than that of mother and
child. From the formal portraits of the old masters to the macho football
player mouthing the words "Hi, Mom" to the television camera—these ties
transcend time and space. Even our Savior laments his rejection by his Jewish
brethren, using the imagery of the mother hen who would gather her chicks
under her wing for protection (Matt. 23:37).

Such sacrificial love and nurturing care begin when a woman has her
pregnancy confirmed or when the call comes from the adoption agency that
a child is waiting—sight unseen, those sacred cords begin to entwine around
her heart drawing her to that child. And those cords will sustain both mother
and child through early years of sleep deprivation and teething and tooth fairy
visits, through adolescent angst and dating and struggles for independence,
through weddings and grandchildren and career choices, right through to the
role-reversal of mother and child that so often occurs in old age.

As a daughter, then a mother, then a grandmother, I have experienced all
those precious relationships, felt all the highs and lows that come with each
season in life's journey, and stand to say, triumphantly, I love being a mother.
My children have filled my heart with joy and pride, frustration and fear; they
have evoked prayers of thanksgiving and petitions for protection. And they
have assured me of God's loving presence from generation to generation.

This compilation of stories tracing one mother's journey through
the years is heartwarming for many reasons. First, the stories shine with

authenticity and honesty which mothers of all ages and generations will validate with "How true! I remember when . . ." Second, the stories sparkle with humor and wit in perfect balance with pathos and pain; there is laughter one moment and tears the next. In short, they reflect life in all its complexity for the Christian woman who strives to model a life of faith for her children while juggling all the balls that come with homes and husbands and hopes and dreams. Finally, these are stories written by my own daughter, whose perspective has taught me and whose strength and maturity have amazed me. My heritage is her heritage, embroidered with her own colors and life experiences, grounded on our common shared faith in our Lord and Savior Jesus Christ. He has entwined our hearts forever and I give him praise and thanks. Forgive my slightly biased commendation; you will love this book!

Introduction

This book has been in the works for over six years. Honestly, it was in the works long before I imagined it would ever be in book form. I began blogging when my son Zeke was an infant. My daughter Julia was three at the time, and it seemed like every day brought something newsworthy. I began writing the stories down, for my own memories and for a few family members and friends who occasionally checked in on me to see what new adventures I was having. When I was offered the opportunity to have these stories published, I was overjoyed. It has always been a dream of mine to be a published author. So, I thanked God for the opportunity and accepted the challenge.

Today my son is almost seven and my daughter is ten! I share with you as I would with my closest friends—the highs and the lows of motherhood, and of womanhood in general. These are stories about life as a woman, life as a mother, life as a believer in Christ. It is my hope that the stories that follow will not only entertain you, the reader, but will also challenge, inspire, and encourage you. After all, we are all in this together, girls! What follows is a collage of snapshots from the last six years of my life. These are true stories. I hope as you read them, you will see the big picture.

Children of God

The Lord your God is with you, he is mighty to save.
He will take great delight in you, he will quiet you with his love,
he will rejoice over you with singing.—ZEPHANIAH 3:17

My favorite time of day is when we are tucking the kids into bed. Not just for the obvious relief from duty that it brings. My baby boy and I have a special ritual. After prayer with Daddy and big sis, we go to his room. I put his cuddling blanket up on my shoulder and he buries his little face in it. He pats me on the back. He smiles up at me with his angel face. We stand together and we rock. And I sing. He knows the song. He doesn't know what the words mean yet, but he knows when I sing it that he is safe. He knows that he is loved.

"Sweet boy, sweet Ezekiel Simpson. Mommy and Daddy love you."

One day he will be a big boy and he will outgrow this sacred ritual. The nuzzling will be replaced by a hug and a kiss on the cheek. He'll be too big to hold and stand together and rock. One day he will be a young man who will give me a quick hug while listening to his iPod. But, even if it is when he is sleeping, I will still sing. And he will know he is safe and that he is loved. Loved deeply and dearly, in the way a mother does. I love my precious children more than myself. How could there be a greater love? "Yet to all who received him, to those who believed in his name, he gave the right to become children of God" (John 1:12).

Children of God.

I have thought many times, though I have never said it to my childless friends, that I understood this love that God has for us much better when I became a mother. As children of our own parents, we all can understand being the *recipient* of parental love. Sadly, there are many who have poor examples to follow. But, when I became a parent, I could finally understand the parental perspective in a richer, fuller way.

Maternal love is deep and unconditional. I would never leave my children. I feel their sorrow when they are sad. Because I am a loving mother, I will always do whatever I can to make their lives better. Because I am a loving mother, I also help to hold them down for their immunizations, despite their tears, because I know it is for their ultimate good. There are moments that I want to yell out, "Would you just cool it?" or "Cut that out!" Sometimes my children frustrate me. They struggle for independence only to make bad choices that could have been avoided if only they would have followed my advice. It is an important part of growing up. But that struggle is sometimes hard to witness. I think God occasionally feels that way, too. There are not many people in this world for whom I would sacrifice my life. But for my children—I don't even need to consider it.

My life for theirs, in a heartbeat.

The gravity of this unconditional love has been proven to me again and again, through the years. I remember one occasion, when Zeke was a baby. He had a bad cold and was also teething. He was also constipated. (Trust me, this is important for the story.) At the cusp of mobility, he was pulling up on everything and getting himself stuck in tight places. In other words, he was a real handful. So, that particular morning was spent wiping snot, wiping tears, administering medicine, cleaning medicine off myself when it was sneezed onto my face, massaging his abdomen, rubbing Vaseline on his bottom, helping him get out from under the piano where he got stuck, and so on. And all that was for just one of my children!

By morning naptime, I was ready to wash my hands with Clorox and plop him in the bed. He was not exactly "putting on the cute." But, as it always does, the day passed. And soon enough, it was bedtime. I washed his little face and cuddled him up with his blankie. As he pressed his sweet-smelling, little face into my chest and I felt his little hand resting on my back, my heart was flooded with love and affection for him. And his song began to flow from my lips, "Sweet boy, sweet Ezekiel Simpson. Mommy and Daddy love you." As high maintenance as he may be at times, he is my child.

Oh, how I love him.

I always will.

So it is with God, my friend. No matter how unpleasant or high maintenance you may be at times, remember that your heavenly Father loves you. Take a moment to tell him that you love him too. Sit quietly with him. Rest in his embrace. Bask in his unconditional love. It will warm your heart . . . and his. "How great is the love the Father has lavished on us, that we should be called children of God! And that is what we are!" (1 John 3:1)

2 Confession

It was a chocolate Bundt cake. And she was four years old. The top was covered with powdered sugar. I saw the first evidence of foul play when I opened the refrigerator door. There were four dents in the top of the cake, in the shape of tiny fingers. The rim of the cake plate, which had only hours earlier been dusted evenly with a thick blanket of white, now had a naked line running around it. This kind of damage could only have been done by an eager finger. Powdered sugar is so pretty. Powdered sugar is hard to resist.

Powdered sugar is hard to conceal.

Julia didn't realize it would stick to her like pollen. As she entered the kitchen, I had to hide my secret delight at seeing her face. She had a ring of white around her mouth. Her lips were white. She had even managed to get a little powdered sugar inside her left nostril. Something must have stirred in her heart, because she came to me to confess the truth.

"Mommy," she began, as a little puff of white came from her nostril. "I ate some of the powdered sugar off of your cake."

I had to listen as if I had no idea. After all, this was unsolicited honesty. This was confession. And it was sweeter than any powdered sugar on the planet. I looked right past her sugar-covered lips and reacted as if this were the first I had heard of it.

"Thank you for telling me the truth, Julia," I answered. Then I wrapped her in a tight embrace, full of pride and thankfulness for this child. After all, she didn't have to tell me.

Of course, I knew all along, just by looking at her. But, there was something so precious about her honest, self-initiated truthfulness . . . it was an endearing moment for me.

I believe it is for our heavenly Father as well.

Being raised in a Protestant family, confession was not often the focus in our worship services. Every so often we would all recite together the traditional words of congregational confession, "Forgive us for the wrong things we have done and the good things we have left undone." But this is very general and easy to say. How many times have we heard a half-hearted apology from one child to another?

Parent: "Say you're sorry."

Child: (Scowl) "Sorry."

This type of apology is not nearly as meaningful as the ones that come from the heart. "I am so sorry that I . . . would you please forgive me?"

We all could use a little more confession.

I have never gone to a chiropractor, but I have seen my father and others I have known benefit greatly from an adjustment. When things are misaligned, there is pain and discomfort. We are not able to be productive in this state. A chiropractor is able to move things back into alignment. This process is not always painless, but it almost always results in relief and renewed productivity. Confession is sometimes painful. But getting back into proper alignment with God is pivotal to our purpose and our ministry.

One of my favorite scriptures is taken from Psalm 51: "My sacrifice, O God, is a broken spirit; a broken and contrite heart O God, you will not despise."

God knows what our week looked like. He knows if we are feeling hatred in our heart towards someone. He knows if we yelled at our spouse or spoke harshly to our children. He knows about the times that we turned to the refrigerator to bring us peace when a prayer would have been much more beneficial. He knows if we gossip about other people in the church pews or fill our minds with filth on television. God is not fooled by our church clothes. So we may as well confess our failings to Him.

After all, he can see our powdered sugar-covered faces.

3 The Waiting Place

My one-year-old son, Zeke, has a developmental delay. He has made tremendous progress—first learning to sit, then roll, and now transition from his stomach to sitting up. Yet, he still hasn't crawled. He gets into position . . . he reaches . . . and then . . . (sigh) he falls forward. I am tempted many times to move his little legs for him. I can manipulate his arms and legs so that it seems like he is doing it, but the motion is not coming from him yet. This is so frustrating.

I hate waiting.

However, manipulating the result we want is not the best solution. After all, who wants a wedding proposal resulting from an ultimatum? The proposal just isn't authentic. The same is true here. Crawling needs to be Zeke's accomplishment. I do believe that when his brain is ready for that next step, he will make the connection. That moment will be just the right time. Then, he'll own his crawling. It will be his. There will be no stopping him.

We are a society of "right now." As Americans, even more than other people, we are used to having things when we want them. We are the inventors of the culinary genre known as "fast food." After all, who has time to make a sandwich? (Although, when you really think about it, we actually wait a lot longer in the drive-through line than it would have taken to make a sandwich at home.) But we think fast food is faster. We don't know how to wait. Not gracefully, at least. I commented on this to a friend earlier this week, while waiting for microwave popcorn to finish popping. Remember the old days when we actually had to heat oil on the stove for popcorn? Now it takes two and a half minutes from start to finish—and we are pacing. It seems that when it comes to our getting what we want, any wait is too long. And yet, we are encouraged to "wait on the Lord." Jesus did precisely that. "You see, at just the right time, when we were still powerless, Christ died for the ungodly" (Rom. 5:6).

God waited for the right time. A time when his people were starving for a Savior. A time when his master plan would be completed. A time when he would redeem us all to himself. The right time. No sooner, no later. His beautiful story had to unfold in the way it was designed. He waited for centuries to undo the damage that was done in the Garden.

He wasn't just waiting to see how it would turn out. Surely, God knew that every generation after Adam would be marked by sinfulness. He knew we would never get it right. He knew what would be required. What if he had just jumped to it? Couldn't he have sent the Savior earlier and avoided a lot of grief? But we would have missed out. We would have missed out on all the stories of faith. We would have missed out on seeing God's faithfulness, from generation to generation, leading up to his most generous and loving act.

So, we need to follow his example. We need to wait on the Lord. You see, there are lessons to be learned in the waiting. It's all part of the package.

Not too long ago, I thought I had cancer. In case you have never been there before, let me tell you, it is a strange and unique place to be. The drama started when a routine trip to the ear, nose, and throat doctor revealed that I have an enlarged thyroid. "Could be nothing," the doctor said, "but just in case . . . let's get an ultrasound." So I did. The ultrasound revealed a nodule. Next step, blood work and a needle biopsy, which I waited three weeks to have. I had the biopsy, which was actually not as bad as I thought it would be. Really it was more scary than painful. I thought the biopsy would be the hard part. Turns out, it was not. The hard part?

Waiting.

I waited a week for the results. It was the longest week of my life. The doctor assured me that cancer was not likely. If it were cancer, the odds were in my favor that it would not be "the bad kind." But, there are four kinds. The chances reminded me of Russian roulette. Scary stuff.

I had an army of people praying for the best result. But there were moments when the doubts crept in. After all, I knew too well that bad things happen to good people. The world is full of good people who have faced life-threatening illnesses with varying results. God chooses to heal some of them in this life. Some of them he chooses to heal in the Resurrection. Stuff happens.

So, I waited. But I did not wait passively. While I waited, I prayed—for myself and for my family. And I lived intentionally—choosing to be fully present for my husband, my children, and my friends. I decided within my heart that whatever happened, it would be okay. (And it did, in fact, turn out to be okay.)

During that week of uncertainty, my brother shared a verse from Scripture with me from *The Message* version of the Bible: "Give your entire attention to what God is doing right now, and don't get worked up about what may or may not happen tomorrow. God will help you deal with whatever hard things come up when the time comes" (Matt. 6:34 *The Message*).

Good advice when you find yourself in the waiting place.

Diving In

She wanted to do it. It was all her idea. But as soon as she stepped out onto the board, we knew it wasn't going to happen. Her body started shaking and she just sat down. "You can do it, J!" we cheered. With mommy on one side of the board and little brother looking on, she inched her way closer to the edge. She could see her daddy, arms outstretched in the water below, poised to catch her.

"Jump!" Michael said. "I've got you!"

It couldn't have been safer. It was her moment, it seemed. The moment of truth. We held our collective breath. And held it. And held it. And, then we had to breathe. In the end, her fear got the better of her. As she walked back and came down from the stairs, she started to cry. Her tears were a mix of disappointment, self-consciousness, and shame.

"I guess I'll never do it," she lamented.

Isn't that just such a perfect analogy for the way we live sometimes? How many times have I passed up an opportunity, set aside my dreams, or backed out of things because the fear got the better of me? We were created for the glory of our Father. Yet, I am convinced that Satan uses our own fears to convince us that we are less than we are. We blame him for the bad things that we do ("The devil made me do it!") but what about the good things that we don't do? Is there room in our theology for "The devil talked me *out* of it?" I think there is. When fear slips in we say: "What will people think?" "What if I fail?" "I could never do that." Then, my friends, he has got us where he wants us.

Once upon a time, I thought about pursuing a career in music therapy. This is a field that uses all the gifts I possess: musical talent, knowledge of musical repertoire, love for children, and a desire to help people. But, it meant graduate school. That would mean taking the graduate school admission tests (I hate tests). That would mean more studying (what if I am not up to it?). If I were accepted (and what if I weren't?) into a program, that would mean years of part-time school (can I keep it up long enough?), driving back and forth (have you seen the price of gas?), and an internship (scary!). I hung the idea up on my invisible bulletin board of retired dreams.

My husband is my best supporter. He is incredibly inspiring. He dreams big, and he doesn't back down. Several years ago he wrote on his office white-board, "Melanie's Melody." He explained his idea for my very own business: teaching private voice and piano lessons to homeschoolers.

"Great idea," I said. "But . . ."

Then, I gave him all the reasons it would not work. Does any of this sound familiar? Last September, I took a leap of faith. I resigned from my safe and cozy church ministry job to make Melanie's Melody a reality. And guess what. The students started pouring in. I needed forty students to pay the bills. At the end of my first month of business, I had forty. Was it a risk? Absolutely. But I took the plunge and the water was fine!

It is easier to stick with what you know. But, what if the beautiful waters below would really be worth the jump? Our heavenly Father waits below us with arms extended, poised to catch us.

"Jump! I've got you!" he calls . . .

Complaining 5

Living a life of gratitude is not always easy. This is a struggle at any age, but particularly when you are a child. The fact is, gratitude, like patience, is best learned through struggle. As with all growth, there are sometimes growing pains. I remember several occasions when Julia had some opportunities for growth.

Julia was three years old at the time. We were about to sit down for lunch and I asked her to go and wash her hands before sitting at the table. She was eager to eat and not happy with this request which would delay her feast by at least, oh forty-five seconds or so. Immediately, her face reflected the great oppression that she felt was being inflicted upon her.

"Ugh! This is the *worst* day of my entire career!" (I have no idea.)

Once Michael and I got up off the floor and stopped laughing, we had a good family discussion about situations that would be legitimately bad, and about the importance of thankfulness. She really seemed to understand.

In the car on the way home from Taco Bell, Julia whined that we were only thinking about ourselves, and not her when we ordered our food. I lovingly reminded her that, in fact, the first order I placed was hers. She really seemed to understand. She smiled sheepishly in her car seat and said, "Oh . . . yeah. Sorry."

On Friday, after spending the morning at her pre-K orientation, then going to the mall to get a birthday present for one of her friends, she complained that the family was not doing anything for her. (This was after Michael and I denied her request for a piece of gum.) We once again reminded her that, in fact, the whole day had been devoted to her. She seemed to understand. She smiled sheepishly and said, "Oh . . . yeah. Sorry."

I have seen this a million times with my children. You can fill an entire day with fun activities just for them, but at the end, say no to a request and suddenly, it is "the worst day." Sometimes I feel like nothing is ever enough. Many times over the past nine years I have said these words:

"Let's just enjoy what we have for a little while before we look for the next thing."

It can be so frustrating! As loving parents, we don't ever seek reimbursement. All we want is a response of gratitude.

Now before you label my sweet daughter a brat, let me suggest that at times we are all like this, in God's eyes. We complain when God doesn't answer our mumbled prayers for a close parking space but forget to thank him for healing us of our illnesses. We complain that he doesn't give us what we *wanted* but forget all the times that he has provided exactly what we *needed*. We are not much more enlightened than the sun-burned Israelites, grumbling in the desert.

"Thanks for the manna, God, but where is the meat?"

So God sends quail. I can imagine one Israelite still muttering, while wiping quail gravy off of his chin,

"What? No dessert?"

We complain about the temporary, worldly needs that we have from time to time, and forget that he has already taken care of our eternal souls. Even if that were all he *ever* did, it would be enough to require our deepest, heart-felt thankfulness. We seem to understand. We honestly think we do understand. But, we so easily forget. If he were to point these things out, *we* would more than likely smile sheepishly and say, "Oh . . . yeah. Sorry."

We are all a little more like three-year-old Julia than we might care to admit. She just says it out loud. So, for now, Michael and I will continue to nurture and teach Julia.

And you and I, well, we can try to do better too.

Taking Time 6

On the way to our church building there is a large billboard on the interstate. On it is a picture of a cute little girl, who appears to be around three years old. She is dressed up like an adult, and you can barely see her sweet, angelic face for the gigantic round adult glasses on her face. The sign reads, "Education Comes First," followed by the name of the advanced day care.

This year, Julia is in pre-K. Unbelievable. I still remember bringing her home from the hospital. She attends the school at our church building. It is a fabulous school and the teachers are exceptional. This year, we were told, it is really important to have the children at school for circle time. Usually, this timing is not a problem. Today it was a major one.

Everything seemed to be against me. Packing lunches for two children, feeding them, dressing them, dressing myself, seemed to take forever this morning. I am not even taking into account my own showering, which I like to do daily when possible.

Breakfast took longer than usual because Julia wanted to mash her strawberries into the cereal milk and make strawberry milk. I yanked it away after a reasonable amount of time.

We can't be late to circle time!

I was in such a hurry to get the kids loaded up, I bumped poor Zeke's head on the top of the car. I quickly rubbed it and buckled him in.

We can't be late to circle time!

I hollered at a man on the road because he didn't use his blinker. "Use your blinkers!" I shouted. Julia laughed.

"Mommy, why are you mad?"

"I'm not mad, Julia . . . *but we can't be late to circle time.*"

We took the tollway, paying the extra money needed to get there quickly. It was backed up for miles. Finally, as I watched the clock roll over to nine o'clock, several miles from the building, I gave in (came to my senses).

"You know what, J? We'll just get there when we get there." We both breathed in deeply. She seemed relieved that the possessed lady whom she fondly knew as Mommy took a much needed chill pill.

I am usually a very rational person when it comes to these things. I am the mommy who goes to Mothers of Preschoolers (MOPS) meetings, trying to learn about priorities and how to make the most of my children's carefree years. I am the mommy who has told Julia's teachers in other preschool years, "We don't really care much about homework at this age. We just want her to have fun." But, something happens to us parents somewhere down the line. We stop protecting the short years of childhood. We buy into the idea that "Education Comes First." We are rushing our children around town like they are little CEOs. We are in such a rip-roaring hurry for our kids to grow up. The public schools are now testing kindergarteners. Parents are panicking. Julia has four-year-old friends who took summer school. Those children should be playing outside in the sandbox. Her friends should definitely be able to eat a leisurely breakfast and make strawberry milk. They have enough years of stress, and homework, and deadlines, and expectations to meet. Why are we parents so eager to thrust our children into the rat race?

I remember the first year I actually took a spring break with the children. It was so delightful! Eye-openingly so. The week was spent reading books, playing on the swing set, preparing birthday invitations, visiting the children's museum. Fun stuff. And you know what happened? I fell in love with my precocious daughter again. I fell in love with my mischievous—but still kisses with his big, open mouth—nineteen-month-old again.

Unfortunately it took a label like "spring break" to encourage me to think outside of the "Wow! Is it naptime yet?" way of thinking. Why is it that we spend most of our lives rushing to what's next? What a huge gift this earthly life is, and yet I believe it is the enemy who fools us into believing that we have plenty of time to spare.

This has been going on in my life as early as I remember.

In fifth grade I remember crying that *all* my friends were getting training bras and starting their periods. (Sorry to any guys who are reading, but believe me when I tell you, it is a big deal for adolescent girls!) I prayed and prayed that I would get mine too. Boy, was *that* misguided!

Then there is the "I-can't-wait-til-I-get-out-of-high-school" stage, followed by the "How-many-more-credits-until-I-get-my-degree?" stage, followed by the "Once-I-find-a-husband . . ." stage. Once Michael and I got married, it wasn't long before we were checking out model homes. And, after the last box had been unpacked in our new house, I launched directly into "Gotta-have-me-some-babies!" We had many date nights that were filled with conversations of "When are we going to have a baby?" "Are *you* ready?" "When, when, *when*?" (That was mostly me.)

In hindsight, where everything is clearer, I wish we would have taken more time to smell the roses, so to speak. If you aren't careful, it can pass you by all too quickly. The upside is that I realize this now and not in a convalescent home!

Even when we feel like our days are moving slowly, our children are growing up around us. Living intentionally can be a way of life. One tangible way that we can make the most of our days is by being generous with the word "yes."

It rained this weekend. I mean, it *really* rained. Buckets. Our back yard is still almost completely drowned in water. Saturday was kind of a lazy morning, with Zeke suffering through a cold and sleeping off and on, and the sun taking a sabbatical of sorts. After working our way through a game of Chutes and Ladders and exhausting the idea of "playing by yourself," Julia commented in passing, "Mommy, I wish I could go out and play in the water, but I don't know where my raincoat is." We do a great job teaching kids to be very practical early in life, you see. We do want them to be responsible adults, after all. But, childhood should also bring adventure, I believe. So, I surprised her.

"Go put on your swimsuit and you can play outside," I said. Her face reflected sheer joy. She raced to her room, put on her suit, and bolted outside. It was the epitome of freedom—not about learning letter sounds, coloring inside the lines, staying clean—just about being a kid. A four-year-old frolicking in the swampy yard. Beautiful.

I recorded her on the video camera for a while. Then she said it. You know what, don't you? "Mommy, come and splash with me!" Ugh. I had just poured myself a cup of coffee and was going to come inside and read, quietly, by myself. To do that would have been fine and very appropriate, since mommies and daddies aren't just here to entertain. I think she expected me to say no. But I didn't. I put on my swimsuit and joined her. We splashed and ran and sat on our bottoms in the water. We laughed and laughed and laughed. It was fun. It was a memory.

We jump so quickly to no with our children. We are so doggone grown-up sometimes that we miss those opportunities to meet our children where they are. In the beauty of childhood. In the glory days of innocence. Before it gets so complicated. Before the invitations to join in cease. Before the bedroom door is closed for girl talk with friends. Before the car keys bring freedom. A friend of mine recently shared with me about a day during which her son had asked her to play in the sprinkler with him. She had a million reasons why *not* to, and she declined his offer. At bedtime, as she tucked him into his little sheets, he talked about the fun he'd had in the sprinkler that morning. She left his room wishing she could have the moment again.

I encourage you today, to measure your nos. But, when possible, give your yeses generously.

Take time today.

Children do grow up so quickly.

A Dose of Reality

If you have been to Target, Walmart, or virtually any mall over the past five years, you have seen the latest craze to hit America. Princess Fever. There are books, CDs, backpacks, lunchboxes, posters, and even panties with the Disney princesses cheerfully displayed. And little girls seem to love them!

When Julia was four, she had a bad case of princess fever. I didn't need to waste a co-pay at the pediatrician's office. The symptoms were crystal clear. She could not get enough of the princesses. She even had a Cinderella birthday party! What's not to love? The stories are very exciting; they each have a villain whom you love to hate, and they always seem to end with the princess winning and getting her way. There is always true love (usually at first sight) involved. Julia loved these stories. What little girl wouldn't?

Several weeks ago, Julia came home from Nana's house with some of my old "Storybook Storyteller" cassette tapes. Some of you may remember those. They begin with "The storybook storyteller presents . . ." These were the original stories, taken from the books of Hans Christian Andersen and others.

We listened to "The Little Mermaid" tape together and talked about the discrepancies between the original story and the Disney movie. At the end of the movie, Ursula, the evil witch, is destroyed and Ariel marries her prince Eric to live happily ever after. It seems that strong-headed young girls can disobey their overprotective fathers and everything will turn out better than before. It appears that Ariel knows best. Her disobedience pays off. Poor, dumb Dad, he just doesn't understand *true love*. Ariel goes around her father, gets her way, and lives happily ever after.

Not so in the original story. The Little Mermaid disobeys her father, signs a deal with the evil witch, and in the end she dies, sacrificing her own life for that of the prince. The happy ending comes from the moral character that develops in the Little Mermaid throughout the course of the story. Thinking only of herself in the beginning, she grows up. She matures. She shows the fruit of true love, because she is willing to lose her own life rather than taking the life of the prince. She gives him up. She watches him marry another. She smiles upon and blesses his wife. She is no longer selfish, as "love does not demand its own way."

This story, like most of the original fairy tales and fables, was written as a life lesson. Disney has now modified the stories, twisting them in order to produce happy endings. Easy endings.

The problem, as I see it, is that real life is not easy. Little girls who disobey their fathers and run away with sweet-talking boys usually end up pregnant, and sometimes alone. Love at first sight wears off after a few weeks. Real love is not an instant feeling. That is called attraction or infatuation. True love honors the commitment, even when there is no castle; even when Prince Charming's crown begins to tarnish. In real life, Prince Charming sometimes loses his job or at the very least, his hair. Real love means *hanging in* when it would be easier to *hang it up*.

I'm not suggesting we do away with fairy tales. These movies are entertaining and sweet, and they are fun to watch. But, as with all entertainment, I do believe that we have the responsibility as parents to talk about these movies with our children. We must help our little girls define what is real and what is not. (And teach our little boys that real girls rarely look like that!) These films can be great opportunities for us to teach what the Bible says about obedience and about love:

> Love is patient, love is kind. It does not envy, it does not boast, it is
> not proud. It does not dishonor others, it is not self-seeking, it is not
> easily angered, it keeps no record of wrongs. Love does not delight

in evil but rejoices with the truth. It always protects, always trusts, always hopes, always perseveres. Love never fails (1 Cor. 13:4–8).

Is princess fever a bad thing? I don't think so. But a good dose of reality never hurts.

8 Perspective

This morning while I was in the bathroom, my one-year-old son came crawling around the corner. I have never been so happy to have my privacy invaded. In fact, I would go even further and say it was a joyful moment for me! You see, Zeke's developmental delay has put him about five months behind in his motor skills. Although he has been crawling since his birthday, this was the first time he actually crawled to look for me. There were many months, when his peers were already crawling around their houses, that I would sit in the bathroom and imagine his rounding that corner, only to return to the living room and find him in the same spot in which I had left him. I was sad for him, since many times he was crying and frustrated not to be able to follow me. It was different with our four-year-old when she was a toddler. With Julia, I was slightly annoyed not to have even a minute of privacy. I remember feeling trapped, and even saying once or twice, "I can't even go to the *bathroom* by myself!" But now this morning, with Zeke, the lack of privacy was joyous.

It is all about perspective. Here are some other tasks to examine in a different light:

> Cleaning the house—bummer—unless you are homeless. I'll bet those people would love to have that chore.

> Washing clothes—bummer—unless you live in a country where you have to do this chore in the river, a mile from home. Then you'd just be thrilled just to have a washer and dryer.

Going grocery shopping—bummer—unless you are eating Spam in a van by the river. Enough said.

Taking care of a needy baby—draining—unless you are struggling with infertility. Then you would stop the world from spinning just for that privilege and joy.

I remember going to the obstetrician for a follow-up visit after our first pregnancy ended in miscarriage. As one of the only not-pregnant women in the crowded waiting room, I sat self-conscious and acutely aware of the emptiness I felt inside my own heart and belly. I watched as women with swollen ankles and aching backs came in and out, grouchy and sullen. I remember vividly seeing a couple exiting with a video cassette of their precious one, growing safely inside the mother's womb. They were so very young and were bickering about something trivial. As I walked a short distance behind them on the way out to the parking lot, I overheard them yelling and even cursing at each other. Tears welled up in my eyes. I thought to myself, "Why can't that be me? They just don't know how lucky they are." The injustice of the situation overwhelmed me and I sat in the car and cried. I decided that if the Lord did give us children of our own, I would never take it for granted. And I loved my pregnancy with Julia, because of that. I even embraced the nausea. It was a welcomed sign that things were going well.

This gratitude through perspective overflows into everything, if we let it. I think it can change our way of thinking and even change our life. Most of our mild burdens can feel much lighter if we try to see them in a different light. My privacy may have come to an end for now. But I know that in only a few short years I will wish I could see that little smiling face rounding the corner again.

It's all about perspective.

9 Friends Forever

If I go back through one of my high school yearbooks, I see about twenty signatures that include the line, "Friends forever!" Suffice it to say, that didn't really work out.

I have never been a very good girlfriend. One big reason is that, unlike a majority of women, I don't enjoy talking on the phone. I literally cringe when it rings. This began when I was very young. I had a friend in middle school who was very enthusiastic about the phone. She called all the time. She called me through high school. She called me when I was home from college. Literally, I would walk in the door for Christmas break and the phone would ring. It was a nuisance. See? Bad friend. Michael teases me about being afraid of the phone. Truth is, there is no fear involved. I just don't enjoy it.

I am also not big on hanging out. When I have a day off, Michael will sometimes suggest, "Why don't you call up a girlfriend and go see a movie?" But, with the exception of one or two friends, I would just prefer to be alone. Besides, I like to go to movies by myself. I struggle not to fall into the trap of being a loner. This has always surprised people who think they know me. In a social situation, I have always been the life of the party. My personality allows me to make friends fairly easily . . . but keeping those friendships going? That's always been tough for me. I've been all right with maintaining just a few close friendships, but many have fallen to the wayside. Of my six bridesmaids from a decade ago, I remain friends with only a couple.

A few years ago, a wise woman from our congregation gave some advice to the young women of the church on a video:

"Get yourself some girlfriends because you're gonna need 'em!"

This tendency has become even truer as the years have gone by, particularly once I became a mother. I remember one day when Julia was only about three weeks old. She was crying nonstop. I was trying to nurse, but was incredibly insecure about it. I felt terrible. I was depressed. My mom wisely suggested that I call a friend.

"But I have you," I told her.

"I am here to help you," she said, "but you need to call a friend who has young children. I don't remember much about this!" she said.

So I did. I called my friend Laurie. She listened to my concerns and gave me some words of reassurance. She also recommended a book that she had found helpful with her babies and even had it shipped to me in the mail. It was a moment that I will never forget. Because I like to give the impression that I have everything under control, this was a big step of maturity for me. Calling a friend meant admitting that I needed help. And, oh boy, did I need the help. I reached out, and I was blessed by it.

Now that the kids are bigger, there are other issues that arise. I have a somewhat regular lunch date with my friend Staci during the school year. Somehow, by God's grace, we have ended up walking similar roads with our children. Having someone to confide in is such a blessing. Sometimes we pray for each other. Sometimes we just listen to each other. We cry when we need to and we laugh a lot.

I do need friends. But realizing that truth is the easy part. Taking, absorbing, receiving is easy. I need to learn to be there when they need me. Sometimes that means dropping a card in the mail. Sometimes, it means picking up the phone when I might prefer to stay in the bed reading quietly. And you know what? I'm trying. And here's why. I have a daughter, and she is watching me. I want her to have deep friendships with other girls. I want her to know what being a friend means. I want her to see me reciprocating concern and love. I want her to practice sacrificial love.

In the Old Testament, we read about one such friendship. David and Jonathan loved one another with a deep, agape love that is extremely rare these days. We are surrounded by fair-weather friends and friendships of convenience. I have fallen into those categories myself. But, at this stage of life, I want to do better. I want Julia to see me reaching out . . . and holding on.

This weekend, Michael went out of town to visit friends (two of his six groomsmen—FYI—he is still close to five of them). My natural tendency would be to stay locked inside, tuck the kids in promptly at eight, and then watch TV alone in the living room. But, instead, I hosted a girls' night, inviting several of the younger women from church over for games and food. We sang karaoke! I even broke out my chocolate fountain, in which we dipped strawberries, cake, and a variety of other yummy treats. Neither of these activities would have been fun alone. And one of them would have been downright disgraceful alone. We laughed and sang and ate. You know what? It was a blast.

When it was bedtime for the kids, Julia came in to say goodnight. As she held my hand and pulled me into the corner of the dining room, it was obvious she had something important to tell me. I honestly thought she was going to ask me to save her some chocolate for the next day. But, this was not a request at all. It was an observation.

"Mommy, you have a lot of friends! I am proud of you!" she said.

I could have talked to her about how there is more to having friends than just throwing a party. But, in that moment, I was proud of myself too.

"I'm trying to, J."

Friends forever? I don't know. But, this party is a really good start.

Measuring Up

When I was in kindergarten, my class participated in a Christmas parade. We rode on a beautifully decorated float dressed as Christmas flowers. I was chosen to be a poinsettia. Seated next to me was another child, also a poinsettia. Our mothers were in charge of making our costumes. Mine was beautiful and full of fluffy, green petals. My neighbor's petals were smaller, and she had fewer of them. I will never forget her leaning over, probably through her own insecurity, and whispering, "Your flower is too big!" I remember it like it was yesterday. I was self-conscious and sad the rest of the parade. I should tell you at this point that my mother was an excellent seamstress. She was also a perfectionist when it came to projects such as this one. I am quite certain now, as an adult, that the other girl had a case of leaf envy. Even though mine was probably the better of the two costumes, I wished that mine were smaller, more average. I just wanted to fit in.

Middle school was full of other experiences like that. Being a pleasantly plump young lady, I never saw drill team as an option for me. But, I joined the pep squad so I could be part of the popular crowd. That group never included me in its social events, though, and after time, I resigned myself to hanging out with the choir and band kids. Some girls dated football players. I dated a saxophone player. I was happy and accepted in that group of kids, but I still longed to measure up. I wanted to be popular. Just like most people, I have experienced moments of rejection. I have had boyfriends dump me for other girls. I have run for offices that I didn't win.

"Be a good judge . . . vote for Fudge!" (They didn't.) These are the moments when you wish you could just blend in, if not completely disappear.

As it turned out, my class did appreciate me for not blending in, and I was elected by my peers to offer the benediction prayer at our high school graduation. This was the beginning of a new era of confidence and a renewed sense of purpose in my identity as a Christian.

These days, for the most part, I am a self-assured, confident woman. I have learned to roll with the punches, absorb some punches, and punch back when necessary. But, being a parent has opened up some of those same insecurities again.

I will never forget my first official parent-teacher conference. I have visited with Julia's teachers every year in an informal way, but when she was in pre-K, her teacher and I sat down for a meeting.

"Julia is very bright . . . she has great potential," the teacher began.

Then, we discussed some of Julia's "areas for growth," shall we say? There was nothing discussed that was new to me. She needs more self-discipline. She can be overpowering to some of the other kids with her dominating personality and occasional moodiness. Those were very accurate observations. But, it's hard to hear anything less than "she's just perfect from head to toe!" And, most of all, it's hard not to take even the most constructive criticism personally. It can leave you questioning:

"Does my child measure up?" and more importantly, "Does my child *perceive* that she measures up?"

It all depends on what measuring tool we are using, doesn't it?

There will always be kids who do more homework. There will always be kids who have nicer clothes. There will always be kids who move up the reading list faster. There will always be kids who get invited to all the play dates. But I want Julia to know that she measures up by the most important standard . . . because she is a child of God. She measures up because Jesus picked up the slack for her at Calvary. There is nothing that she can do to add to that. Nothing she can do to lose that. As parents, despite our own insecurities and the baggage that we carry from our own experiences, we have to remember that our children were not created in *our* image, but in the image of God.

So I tuck her in at night and tell her, "You are the best little girl in the whole, wide world." After all, she is a daughter of the Most High God.

That is more than enough.

11 When Sympathy Falls Flat

The year that my husband's mother died, his dear family friend also passed away. One day, shortly after his mother's funeral, a card came in the mail, addressed to Michael. We could tell by the shape of the envelope that it was probably a sympathy card. Prepared to read some words of comfort, we took the card out and opened it. Inside were these words:

"First your mother and now your family friend. What next?"

No, I am not kidding. It is quite funny now, but at the moment the sentiment was not what the doctor ordered. I should say that something good did come from that horrendous card, as it has been referenced at least fifty times since that day by various family members and friends and has brought about many chuckles. The card was well-intended, but missed the mark.

Recently, we have been cleaning out the garage. Among the treasures we unearthed were a stack of sympathy cards from our first miscarriage in 2001. As I reread them all, I could remember all the emotions that were swirling around me during that time. I was in such a dark place during those days. In the stack, there were some precious cards, poems written by others who had experienced the same loss before, and many, many cards of encouragement from our church family. Some of the cards, although sent with the best intentions, really just exacerbated the hurt. Instead of strengthening my faith, they made me question my faith. I had a hard time accepting them as a gift.

Here are some of the phrases that I found in my own stack of cards:

- Remember, there is a reason for everything.
- God has his reasons.
- It was God's will.
- God won't give you more than you can handle.
- One day you will understand why this happened.
- At least it happened before you really loved the baby.

True, everything happens for a reason. The reason is that we live in a fallen world. The laws of nature are in play here, and the perfection of paradise has not yet been restored since the Fall of man. God has allowed there to be evil and darkness in the world. It was not his original intention when he created us. Sin opened the door to these consequences. God loves us enough to give us free will. Just as he didn't create us to be robots, he also allows sadness to touch us during our earthly lives. But, I believe that God is sad too. One day He will come back and make everything right and perfect again.

"God will not give you more than you can handle."

I wish I had a nickel for every time I hear this sentence. I do not believe that there is some heavenly Richter scale measuring how much someone can handle. Sometimes it does feel like more than you can handle. The fact of the matter is, grief stinks. But I believe this with all my heart—he will stick with you until you are through it. Maybe one day we will understand why these things happen to us. My hunch is we won't. But honestly, in heaven I don't think we will care anymore. We won't care to or need to know the reasons. It may just be that "poop happens" (paraphrase mine). I do believe that God can bring good out of situations that seem bad to us. After all, he is in the business of redemption!

As for the last statement—well, that is just ignorant. We loved that baby from the moment we saw the red line on the pregnancy test. By week nine I had already finished reading two books about pregnancy and was nearly through the baby name book.

My theology on suffering changed drastically during my own experiences with loss. Here is what I learned about giving comfort: if you don't know what to say, the best thing to say is exactly that.

"I don't really know what to say, but I am here and I care about you."

Don't try to wax theological. Sometimes the best words are the simplest. Or silence. It's good too. Remember the point at which Job's friends ceased being comforting? It was when they opened their mouths and tried to explain what was happening. They did their best work sitting silently with Job in the ashes.

Here were some of the most comforting phrases in my collection of cards:

> We love you.
> God be near.
> I am here for you when you are ready to talk.
> I have been there too.
> The pain and loss that you feel is real, but it will lessen in time.
> Remember the essence of his promise: he is faithful and will carry you through.

It may not be fair, but bad things do happen to good people. So, we may as well prepare ourselves to offer comfort in the most comforting way.

Child–Raising and other Tales of Terror

It has been thirty–four years since the announcement was made. But I still remember the two sentences. They went like this:

"Mrs. Fudge, please come to customer service. We have your daughter here."

The funny thing is, I cannot remember how we got to that point. I imagine I saw something cool and wandered off to investigate it. My mom was probably distracted with the list of things to buy or thinking through the week's menu plan. Somehow, we got to that point. And the announcement was made. I remember my mom rushing up to the customer service counter to retrieve me. Her face reflected a mix of relief and anger and love, an emotional cocktail only a mother could experience. I don't think she had been looking for me long. But, when you are the mother, a minute can feel like a lifetime.

Can we all just agree that raising children is scary—most of the time? The first year of my children's lives I felt like my job was just keeping them alive. I remember watching them sleep as infants, certain that if I stopped looking, they would stop breathing. This was especially true with Julia because she made a strange, snorting sound when she slept. I just knew she was close to the end. She wasn't. Since then, I have had many experiences of panic as a mother. Julia and Zeke have both given me at least one moment that is forever burned into my memory.

Julia's happened on a routine visit to the endocrinologist. Her doctor's office is on the fifth floor of an eight-story building. There are six large elevators in the lobby that transport the hundreds of people who visit up and down every day. She was six years old, and was deeply engrossed in her favorite, new hobby—reading. The appointment was over and we were making our descent from the fifth floor. I was holding Zeke's hand as we stepped off onto on the floor of the lobby. Julia was standing behind us reading her book. I turned around at the exact moment that she looked up from her book . . . just as the doors to the elevator were shutting. *"Mommy!"* she cried as I watched her face disappear behind the stainless-steel metal doors. Zeke looked shocked. I went numb from head to toe.

Quickly, I pushed the button, in the hopes that it had not been responding to a call, but would instead open up again where we were standing. It did not. I watched the dial above the elevator going down. I pushed the button a little harder. I was beginning to panic. Our steel chariot returned and opened, and I was preparing to grab Julia off and hug her tightly. The doors parted to reveal . . . an empty elevator.

Desperation.

I found a security guard and calmly (yeah, right) told him my story. He put out a call on his walkie-talkie and told me not to worry. They would find her. The next five minutes were some of the longest of my life. I felt sick. My mind was racing. I began to imagine the worst. My precious baby. What if Julia were gone for good? I thought about all the recent annoyances that I had felt with her: her messy floor, her endless chattering, her whining at breakfast time. It all seemed so superficial now. I prayed. I pleaded with God.

"Please, God. Just let her be all right. I will do anything." And I would have.

The security guard's voice broke through my silent prayers. "Ma'am, we found her. She got off on the basement level and they are bringing her back up to you now."

"Thank you, God," I whispered under my breath.

When the doors opened with my girl standing there, it was as if we had not seen each other for years. After I *yanked* her off the elevator, the three of us stood and hugged. I think we all cried. Even the small crowd of strangers around us was relieved!

On the way home, we had a great opportunity to talk about elevator safety and to get a plan ready in case that ever were to happen again. "Stay on the elevator," she repeated back to me. "If you have to get off, go to the lobby." Exactly. This was one of those lessons that you never think to teach until you are in the middle of the crisis. It has been three years since that incident, and we still hold hands getting on and off elevators. I imagine we always will. Well, at least until she is twenty-one.

Zeke's scary moment happened when he was about eighteen months old. I was convinced that he had swallowed something nonedible. Trouble is, I had no idea what it was. First there was gagging and coughing, followed by my frantically trying to see what was in the back of his throat. Then he swallowed and immediately moved into hysterical crying. He drank some milk and was finally able to be soothed, but even after several hours of uneventful and happy playing, I still went to bed that night with an upset stomach. There's the inevitable war within your parent heart—emergency room or no emergency room? The logical part of your brain says, "Obviously he is breathing fine and happy. The object will just 'pass' on its own. No point in paying a seventy-five dollar co-pay to be told to 'watch his poop.'" Then there is the emotional side (slightly stronger in me) which says, *"Take him to the ER! He's gonna die!"*

Well, needless to say, he did manage to stay in the land of the living. A follow-up appointment at the doctor the next morning confirmed that the logical part of my brain was indeed correct. (It almost always is.)

These little episodes are the wake-up calls of life. It is in these moments that we are reminded just how precious and fragile life really is, and how every moment with our children is a sacred one to treasure. Too often we get into the rut of day-to-day life. And we forget.

I know in my heart this is not the last scare we will have with either of the children. And my mom informs me that this fear does not go away for parents. She says, "Just wait until they can drive."

Raising children is lots of fun. When it isn't terrifying.

13   Winds of Change

I have told you these things, so that in me you may have peace.
In this world you will have trouble. But take heart!
I have overcome the world. —John 16:33

And surely I am with you always, to
the very end of the age. —Matthew 28:20

When our son was eighteen months old, we had him evaluated at Texas Children's Hospital. We were not strangers to
the language of delay, but needed to be sure there was not more going on.
Thankfully, the testing ruled out some very scary diagnoses. Michael and I
were both a little disappointed however, that the doctor did not say, "Oh,
this is just much to do about nothing," or "He will totally grow out of this!"
She prescribed physical and speech therapy—a private facility, instead of the
governmentally funded one that we currently work with. She also ordered a full
battery of tests—blood work (six vials, poor Zeke!) and an MRI or magnetic
resonance imaging of his brain.

I was doing okay with all this until I read all the materials that the social
worker had packed into a large, manila envelope. Absorbing page after page
about children with "special needs," support groups, special education, and
the like was a little more than I could process at one time. I cried a little and

packed it away for another time. I can deal with this "thing" in bites, but not in its entirety just yet. There are so many questions yet to be answered.

Yet change is coming for us. There is definitely a stirring in my soul that I "ain't seen nothing yet" or more profoundly, that this is all going to unfold to something which later I will look back on and pinpoint as the moment I grew, in a different way than I ever imagined I would. I didn't ask for any of this, but it does seem to fit. All that I have gone through in my life has led me here.

If I hadn't had my heart broken in college, I wouldn't have met Michael.

If I hadn't met Michael, I wouldn't have had Julia and Zeke, or the miscarriages.

If I hadn't had miscarriages, I wouldn't have the perspective to know that it is better to have children who need a little help, than not to have them at all.

If I hadn't had a child who needs a little extra help, I wouldn't . . .

Mixed in with the reading material from the social worker was an article written by a mother with an autistic child, Jessy, who is now an adult. The mother is Clare Claiborne Park. Obviously, as the mother of a child with autism, she has had a very tough road to travel. Yet, within her memoirs, which she published, was this beautiful quote in which I found great encouragement:

> This experience we did not choose, which we would have given anything to avoid, has made us different, has made us better. Through it we have learned the lesson of Sophocles and Shakespeare—that one grows by suffering. And that too is Jessy's gift. I write now what fifteen years past I would still not have thought possible to write: that if today I was given the choice, to accept the experience with everything that it entails, or to refuse the bitter largesse, I would have to stretch out my hands— because out of it has come, for all of us, an unimagined life. And I will still not change the last word of the story. It is still love.

Indeed, that is the first word of my story. And that love will anchor us, when the winds come.

14 | Fighting the Martyr Within

I have been a martyr as long as I can remember. Not a martyr for the faith; the much-less admirable kind. I can roll "no, I didn't want any pie, anyway" off my tongue like water off a duck's back, all the while staring forlornly at the empty pie pan. I try to fight it, as my husband informs me that it is not an attractive quality. Some weeks are just harder than others. A perfect storm was brewing when Michael injured his back. Prime martyr property! During the course of five days of excruciating pain, he took two trips to the ER, one to the doctor's office and had an MRI. I know, poor Michael. But, while he is to be pitied for this, who was keeping the household running? Who do you think?

Moi! What can I say? I am sacrificial.

The first night we realized that there was only one position that he could sleep in to relieve the pressure in his back. This position required me to sleep with my head at the foot end of the bed. I realize this is hard to envision as a reader. Trust me when I tell you, head at the foot end = bad.

After my less-than-restful night, I was up and at 'em with the kids at six. For some sick reason, the Lord has given us rooster children. If they could only crow we might make some money. I quickly worked to get them dressed and fed and occupied so that I could begin the process of helping my patient do the same jobs. Did I mention that my patient is built like a NFL linebacker?

That morning, Michael decided that he needed to go back to the doctor. We had to kick it into gear as fast as we could so that we could get to the doctor's office before the mobs. You see, our doctor only sees patients on a walk-in basis on Fridays. Michael did not think he needed to go on Thursday. So here we were. I knew we were in for a long wait. On the way to the doctor's office cattle call, I had to reschedule dental cleanings that had been planned for both kids that morning.

As we arrived at the doctor's office, the freezing drizzle began falling from the sky, just as I began the slow process of helping Michael get out of the car—one leg at a time, one inch at a time. Drip, drip, drip. The freezing rain fell on my head.

We did get in rather quickly after all, so after loading my patient back into the car, I called and rescheduled the dental cleanings.

Here was the rest of the day:

1. Picked up Michael for a two o'clock MRI appointment.
2. Filled out five pages of paperwork.
3. Sat in waiting room until four-thirty.
4. Took Michael home and immediately got to work making dinner.
5. Cleaned up kids and dinner mess.
6. Gave both children a bath.
7. Folded a load of laundry.
8. Tucked the kids into bed.
9. Left home at eight-forty-five to do our weekly grocery shopping and pick up Michael's prescription, in the freezing drizzle.
10. Brought in and put away groceries by myself at nine-forty.
11. Fell into bed around eleven, once again with my head at the foot end.

Thank you so much for listening.

Now, the Melanie of the past (last week—well, actually yesterday, too) would have been loudly sighing, huffing around the house, and mumbling things about wishing someone would hurt *my* back so I could rest. Truth be told, I did a teeny bit of that. But, I reigned it in every time, folks. At ten o'clock

I really wanted to scream and cry and say mean things . . . but I didn't! I am learning how to control myself—late bloomer, but whatever. So, instead I took a bubble bath. I lit my new scented candle and sat in the tub in the dark, listening to the bubbles pop by my head. I recited Psalm 23. I thought about the words to the song "Make Me a Servant," and mused about how much I enjoy singing it, and hate actually doing it. I asked God to help me do better. I inhaled. I exhaled.

I returned from the bathroom refreshed and relaxed. I was even able to smile at Michael. I fought the martyr within. And this time, I won.

That's one small step for women. One giant leap for *this* woman.

KO in the Fifth Round

This chapter is not about boxing. It is about one of the trickiest parts of parenting. No, not potty training. Maybe the *second* trickiest. Discipline. You see, at some point or another, even the sweetest, most obedient children realize that they are not robots. They can think and speak for themselves. And they do. And the battle for authority begins. It is nothing new or alarming—it's the stuff you see on reruns of the *SuperNanny*. There was a period of time not too long ago that, "No, I don't *want* to take a nap!" and "Then you must not love me!" were heard almost daily at my home. Sometimes I still have no clue how to respond in the most beneficial way. Other times, I am sure of myself.

Julia was fighting bedtime. Oh, initially she went down easily at eight-fifteen. But within five minutes of being in her room, the "fun" started. Notice that fun is in quotes. She snuck out of her room and peeked around the corner. We calmly told her that we could, in fact, see her, and that she was to go back to her room. I escorted her to her room and tucked her back into bed with a clear warning not to come out again. Did she heed the warning? What do you think? Two, yes, two minutes later, we saw her tiptoe around the corner, this time hiding under the dining room table.

Thus began the battle for authority.

Round One—(Ding!)—Julia sneaks out.

Warning: "Julia, do not come out again or you will lose the teddy bear."

Round Two—(Ding!)—Julia sneaks out.

Consequence: Bye-bye, teddy bear.

Round Three—(Ding!)—Julia sneaks out.

Warning: "You will get four swats on your bottom if you come out."

Round Four—(Ding!)—Julia sneaks out.Consequence: One, two, three and (ouch!) four.

She cries and we all go to bed (it's almost ten at this point) and then, oh yes, my friends.

Round Five—(Ding!)—We hear footsteps on the kitchen tile as Julia sneaks out on a reconnaissance mission called "Project Bring Teddy Bear Home." Consequence? Daddy goes in, takes away teddy bear *and* kitty toy, plus, one more swat on the bottom.

I lie in the bed listening for her footsteps. Surely she would surrender now. And after five rounds, and nearly two hours, she did.

Winner? Parents!

We could have pretended not to see her or waited until she fell asleep under the dining room table and carried her to bed. There have been times that I have let things slide. But, this time, we had set out clear expectations. And once the bar was set, we could not compromise. Would it have been easier just to let things be? Certainly! But, if our kids find a way to trump us at age four, Lord help us at age fourteen! So, we prevailed. We had to.

I can still remember the discipline that I received as a child. In the Fudge home, spankings were rare, reserved for willful disobedience and disrespectful language or behavior, otherwise known as my specialties. These attitude adjustments were done in the laundry room of our house. Being of the strong-willed variety, I visited the laundry room more frequently than my little brother. Jeremy was a parent's dream. He was blessed with a sensitive conscience, and would get to the repentance stage quickly. It was punishment enough for him just knowing that he had disappointed Mom and Dad. He was tender-hearted. I, on the other hand . . . well, I had an obsession with getting the last word. (Some would say that I have not outgrown this. To those people, I say, "Oh yes, I have. So there.")

I remember one occasion in particular that will paint a picture for you. I was about seven years old. My mother had scolded me or displeased me in some way and I responded by shaking my fist at her behind her back. She saw me with the eyes in the back of her head and warned, "Don't you shake your fist at me!" So, when she turned around (I was a slow learner) I shook my elbow at her. Funny, huh? I thought it was hi-la-ri-ous! My mom did not. That episode ended in the laundry room.

I only remember a couple of laundry room visits, although I am quite sure there may be notches carved into the washing machine. Interestingly, the most effective consequence that my parents ever imposed was when I was about fourteen years old. I was being sassy, as we called it in the South. My consequence was a creative one. Daddy brought my Bible to me along with a yellow highlighter pen. He told me that I was to read the book of Proverbs and mark every verse that mentioned children and parents. Guess what I found out? Let's just say, there was a *lot* of yellow. But I learned a lot. It stuck with me. Within the first ten chapters, I realized that in the language of Proverbs, I was patterning the fool and not the wise man. Some would argue that having your child read the Bible should not be associated with punishment. I would say to them, "It worked for me! So there."

Parents can debate the best method of discipline until the cows come home. The most important trio, as I see it, is this:

1. Pick your battles wisely.
2. Once you have picked, you must win the battle.
3. Discipline must always be done in love.

We will all make mistakes as parents from time to time. We will let things slide that we should not. We will fight sternly for things that really don't matter much in the long run. We have to give ourselves permission to make mistakes from time to time. As a new mother, I asked a wise therapist at our church, "How do I know if I am being a good mother?" I was expecting a check list of some sort or maybe some scripture. Her answer was short and sweet, and I will never forget it.

"If you are asking yourself that question, you are on the right track."

This simple sentence filled me with confidence. So, as the battles arise, and they will, we pray for wisdom, act in love, and stand firm with confidence. And we rest in the knowledge that loving discipline communicates to our children that we love them, even if they don't see it that way in the moment. We can always remind them that we too are under a higher authority. And we can model obedience for them, as we submit to God's leadership in our own lives.

"The Lord corrects everyone he loves, just as parents correct their favorite child."

That is chapter three, verse twelve, from the famous book of Proverbs, one of my favorite books in the Bible. (Did you catch that part about the favorite child?)

Thanks, Dad.

So there.

Resolutions 16

New Year's Eve—six-thirty.

Julia informs the family that her naughty days are in the past. "I am not going to be naughty at all in the New Year."

This is very refreshing news to her mother, who just hours earlier had to drag her out of the church building, while she yelled, "*No*, Mommy. I don't want to go with *you*!" Michael and I only exchange knowing looks, smile and nod.

"That's great, J."

New Year's Day Morning—eight-forty-five.

Julia is reprimanded for speaking disrespectfully to her mother.

So, let's see here . . . that would be just over fourteen hours of success in a New Year's resolution. But, I don't think Julia is alone here. How are you doing with yours?

Michael and I talked today about the whole resolution thing, and why it is usually very short-lived in our house. My excuse? I tend to be an extremist. All or nothing. So, my goals are usually too big to achieve—at least in the short time frame I allow for them.

I want to lose the fifty pounds I have put on during my pregnancies. Last year I wanted to lose forty. I gained ten. And, this is why: all or nothing. I looked into joining a commercial weight-loss program. But, it was too expensive and way too strict. One ounce of cheese on nachos?? Maybe if you are a mouse! Give me a break. I joined 24-Hour Fitness, but then with the time change . . . you know, it gets dark so early now. And who wants to get up early and go to the gym? Historically, I have not been a great example in resolve.

So this year, I am doing things a little differently. I am getting back into my spinning class, even if I can't win the perfect attendance award. I am going to park a little farther from the door. Occasionally, I will choose the stairs, even if the elevator is not broken. I'll try to take a walk around the block a few times a week. Our fat dog would benefit from this as well. I'll stop feeling compelled to eat dessert after every meal, and maybe save my treat for after dinner only.

I have some spiritual goals this year too. When I feel like I want to gossip or talk negatively about someone, I am going to pray for them instead. This should keep my mouth plenty busy until next year. And maybe if I am using my mouth more for praying instead of eating, I will achieve both of my goals.

I'll let you know.

Saving and Waiting

We are on a new budget. Actually, to be honest, we are stick-ing with a real budget for the first time in our married lives. Part of this budget means that we can stick some money away for a tenth anniversary getaway this summer. We are saving up. Don't get me wrong—it would still be fun if we could just take a wad of cash and leave today, but there is something so wonderful about anticipation.

This is not a new experience for me. When I met Michael, he was serv-ing in the U.S. Air Force. Shortly after we were engaged, he was sent to South Korea for a six-month assignment. For one third of our engagement time, he was literally on the other side of the world. I missed him something awful. In anticipation of our wedding day, I was walking three miles every evening. I walked the same course every day. Along the way, there was a large corn field. At the beginning of our separation, the corn field had just been prepared and the new corn planted. I used to tell myself, "Once the corn is tall, he will be home!" I would have times of sadness walking past the field, feeling that the day would never come. But in the meantime, we waited. And we wrote each other letters. Real letters. On paper. Remember those? We also sent each other tapes in the mail. It was such a treat to hear his voice. And we grew closer, despite the distance. We grew closer at heart. We learned about each other more than we could have if we had been distracted by the physical. I would not trade anything now for that time. And you know what? The corn grew. When fall came—it was such a sweet reunion.

Five years later, we waited together, for the birth of our first child. That last month was so very long. I had my suitcase packed and by the door for weeks. (Why do the books tell you to do that?) The nursery was ready. The thank-you notes for shower gifts were mailed and received. Our daughter was due on March 24. That was the week before Easter. Her coming home outfit was a little bunny Onesie with a cute little bunny-eared cap. Preciousness. Easter came and went. No Julia. An induction date was set for April 4. I remember talking to a dear friend on the phone on the evening of April 1.

"You know, you will probably go into labor now that you have an induction date!" she comforted.

Four hours later, we dusted off the suitcase and headed to the hospital. What a joyful day followed, as we looked into the eyes of our highly-anticipated darling.

There have been many, many more times of waiting. Some happy, some bittersweet.

I remember the five days that my mother and I waited by my grandmother's bedside, wondering which soft, shallow breath would be her last. Those five days were an eternity. They were painful, as we watched helplessly as she drifted away from us. They were beautiful, as we spent the time left holding her wrinkled hand and tenderly touching her silver hair. We started the process of cleaning out her drawers. We discovered pictures, cards, pieces of her history. Mom and I shared our favorite memories. It was a priceless time of waiting. Yesterday, we sang an old "heaven song" at the end of our worship service.

> When the trumpet of the Lord
> shall sound,
> and time shall be no more,
> And the morning breaks eternal, bright and fair;
> When the saved of earth shall gather over on the other shore,
> And the roll is called up yonder, I'll be there.
> ("When the Roll is Called Up Yonder," James M. Black)

The more life I live, the more I look forward to that day. As I become more and more aware of our fragile mortality, the hope of heaven grows inside me.

I hope I will see much more of life before that day. I want to experience the joys of watching my children grow up. I want to share more of this earthly life with my sweet husband. I want to develop deeper and more meaningful relationships with my girlfriends. I want to make a difference for the Kingdom of God.

But I suppose my spirit is saving up even now—waiting for the day when all the waiting will end.

18 Repentance

I decided this morning that I would take the kids to our neighborhood Splash Pad. It is a fun place for them to play in the water, without the risk of drowning. This was our first completely sunny day in four weeks. So, upon deciding this, we all got in our suits and began the ten minute process of layering sunscreen on every inch of my very melanin-challenged children's bodies, followed by a liberal application of mosquito repellent, since Houston has become a swamp in the past two weeks.

We made our way to the Splash Pad only to find that, ta-dah, it was broken. We pushed every stinking button in the place . . . no water. Julia chimed in positively, "Mommy, it's okay. We can just go to the pool!" Neither of the kids can swim independently yet, but I decided that we could stay in the baby pool, which at its deepest reaches one and a half feet. Never mind that the baby pool completely grosses me out. I was willing to make the sacrifice in order to make the kids smile, and not to waste all the sunscreen.

No sooner had we stepped into the baby pool, the lifeguard (who might have been fifteen years old and did not understand the plight of a desperate mom!) blew his whistle.

"Adult Swim! All kids have to leave the pool."

Not thinking that applied to the baby pool, which no adults were swimming in, we stayed where we were.

"Ma'am," he said flippantly, "It's adult swim. That means your kids have to get out of the water too."

This was the moment when my sanity left the building.

I snapped. I mean, I almost heard a literal snapping sound.

"You have got to be kidding me!" I began. I didn't cuss, but I complained. Loudly. I snatched the kids up. I stormed to the car. I squealed my tires like one of the Duke boys and honked the car horn.

"This is a *stupid* place!" I yelled. My children are now looking at me like I am crazy. Rightfully so. Julia meekly peeped from the backseat,

"Mommy, we don't say 'stupid.'"

I went home and called the homeowners association. Very calmly I told my story. The very nice man told me he didn't know about the Splash Pad's being broken, and that the rule about clearing the water for adult swim did *not* apply to the baby pool. "Nanny-nanny-boo-boo," my inner child taunted. The nice man promised to call and let the lifeguards know. I decided not to ask that the lifeguard be fired, by a firing squad. Seemed a little excessive.

So—determined to get something positive out of our day—and to use the already-applied sunscreen and mosquito repellent, we drove to a Splash Pad fifteen miles away, and had a grand time.

What is the point of this long story, you may be asking. This is a terrible story, you may think. Well, my friends, this is a story of redemption. On the way to the new place, I took some deep breaths. I apologized to the children. I explained to them that Mommy acted inappropriately, and that if they were to act that way, they would be sent to their rooms. I asked their forgiveness for yelling. I did not make excuses for the way I acted.

"Whew. You are our real mommy again," said Julia, in a manner suited to someone with a touch of Post-traumatic stress disorder.

On the way home, we passed up the house.

"Where are you going now?" Julia asked.

"We have one more stop to make," I said. We pulled up to the neighborhood pool and Julia went with me to the lifeguard. Amazingly, his head had grown back. There were still teeth marks on his neck . . .

"I want you to know that I am sorry," I said to the teenage boy, who had probably chalked it up to old lady PMS. "I took out my frustration on you, and it wasn't your fault," I continued.

"It's okay," he mumbled.

"No, I was out of line and that is not the example I want to set for my kids. I really am sorry," I finished.

As we walked away, Julia put her arm around me. "Mommy, you did a good thing. This was a good day."

A good day indeed.

The Greater Thing

19

I was leaving for a weekend-long trip. On the morning of my departure, I tried to be very intentional with the time spent with the children. (I generally try to live this way, but find it more in my mind when I am to fly on a plane without them. Kind of like making sure that your life insurance is current.) All I wanted to do was cuddle with them.

"Julia, I have a great idea," I began. "After breakfast, let's go cuddle on the couch and I can read you and Zeke a book!"

Julia thought about it. I could see her mind working even before words came out in response.

"Mommy!" she said with great excitement and a glitter in her eye. "I have a better idea! You can come outside and push Zeke and me on our swings!"

"Well, J, that sounds fun for you, but that really wasn't what I was hoping for. I just want to cuddle and be close to you guys a little while. But—I would be glad to swing you if that would make you happy."

So, I did. After a very short swinging time, we packed up and headed to the elementary school to drop Julia off. And shortly after, I boarded a plane, feeling the loss of my precious cuddle time.

On the plane I reflected—that is so much like our relationship with God. He is our father after all. We are his children. All he wants is for us to have relationship with him—to be in his presence—to spend time basking in his love—to receive his love for us so that we can pass it on. But, just like Julia we so often counter his invitation.

"I have a better idea . . . here's what you could do for me."

Sometimes he allows us to have what we ask for, because he loves us like a father. We do, after all, have free will. But I can imagine how much joy he would feel if, as his children, we said instead, "There are some things I need, Father. But more than those things, right now I really just want to be with you."

By the way, once we got to school Julia said, "Mommy, I wish I would have chosen the cuddle time instead of swinging." Maybe next time she will remember the greater thing.

Maybe I will too.

Night

20

It's two-forty in the morning. I am awakened by a cry, which I immediately recognize as that of my youngest, Zeke. He needs me. As I sleepily stagger into his room, I find him sitting up in his bed.

"What's wrong?" I ask.

"Mama, pweez turn on my night yite."

I do. Zeke pulls his arms up under his head and rolls over to return to sleep. He is happy now.

"Tang too, Mama," he says.

As I make my way back into the bedroom, I reflect on what just happened. It might not have seemed remarkable to an outside onlooker. But it was huge. You see, it wasn't long ago that Zeke's speech delay made it nearly impossible for him to articulate what he needed.

"What do you want, Zeke?"

(tears and babbling)

"I am sorry, honey. Mommy doesn't understand."

At this point, we would start down the checklist:

"Zeke, does something hurt?"

"Do you need to go to the potty?"

"Are you cold?"

"Hot?"

"Thirsty?"

"Scared?"

It could be very frustrating for both Zeke and for us, as Michael and I would try to decipher his needs and wants. That frustration is what made this conversation so remarkable and special. This moment is exactly what I have been writing on his speech therapy paperwork every week for over a year beside the question, "What outcomes would you like to see?"

My answer has always been the same, week after week: "For Zeke to be able to communicate his needs and wants independently." I wasn't looking for *The King's Speech*! Only for Zeke to be able to tell me what was wrong when he woke up in the middle of the night.

This moment was a little miracle. This was the result of much hard work, a great speech therapist (thanks, Ms. Karen!), and the grace of God.

I return to my bed deeply happy and satisfied about what I have just witnessed. I suppose I am ready to face the next obstacle now.

Zeke will have to have eye surgery soon. The patching of his eye has not worked to correct his amblyopia. We faced this same thing with Julia; however, the patching worked for her. Zeke must go to the next stage of intervention. Bless his heart, he always has to go to the next stage. He will be under anesthesia. I am aware of the risks involved in anesthesia and I am fearful for my little boy. Once we make it through the surgery day, we will need to be very cautious during the two week healing period following the surgery. As I reflect on the "what ifs" and worst-case scenarios, I almost forget about the speech victory that just took place. As I lie in the bed, I realize that I am clenching my hands in fists.

"Unclench your fists and go to sleep," I tell myself. But the future seems somehow scarier at night, in the dark, in the silence. And I am anxious.

I had gone to bed anxious, thinking about Zeke, but not about the eye surgery. These days he is almost obsessed with Baby Einstein. It was cute at first. Julia was the same way. She loved to see all the movies and loved playing with her Baby Einstein toys and puppets. But Zeke takes his interest a little further. He talks about Baby Einstein all the time.

"What did we see at Best Buy, Zeke?"

"Baby Einstein!"

"What else did we see?"

"Baby Einstein! Baby Einstein! Baby Einstein!"

"Stop saying things over and over, Zeke." Michael and I remind him of this almost daily. It is impossible to tell if he can help the repetition or not.

My mommy gut is wrenching a bit. Is this just a stage? When he was evaluated by a pediatric neurologist as a baby, we were told there was no autism. But what if this is not just a stage . . .

"Unclench your fists, Melanie, and go to sleep," I tell myself. And I had been asleep—until my two-forty in the morning wake-up moment. Now, even in the afterglow of his speech victory, the worry was beginning to creep back in.

Life is just like this, isn't it? The good is sometimes so tightly wound in with the bad. But we must focus on the good.

Jesus says, "Can all your worries add a single moment to your life?" (Matthew 6:27 NLT).

I roll over and reflect on the words to an old Fanny Crosby song I remember hearing my grandmother sing and play "All the Way My Savior Leads Me" on the piano. I can almost hear her sweet, crackly voice in my head, as I lay very still and imagine the words washing over me like a lullaby.

> All the way my Savior leads me.
> What have I to ask beside?
> Can I doubt His tender mercy
> Who through life has been my guide?
>
> Heavenly peace, divinist comfort
> Here by faith in Him to dwell.
> For I know whate'er befall me
> Jesus doeth all things well.
>
> For I know whate'er befall me
> Jesus doeth all things well.

Slowly, my fists unclench.

21 Words

Julia (upon seeing a beautiful sunset): "Oh my *gosh*, look at the sky!"

Me: "Oh my *goodness*. Goodness. Not gosh."

Julia: "Why can't I say gosh?"

Me: "Because it is awfully close to saying 'God' and that is not respectful. Remember the commandment about not taking the Lord's name in vain? It is just better to stay away from things that are close to that. But, when you are praying, it is okay to say Dear God."

(Silence)

Julia: "Oh, my dear God, look at the sky!"

Me: (groan)

So today, Julia came out with this gem: "Mom, Zeke and I suck!" I was shocked enough (and foolish enough) to ask her to repeat the phrase, which she did.

"Where did you hear that?" I asked in horror.

"Enrique says it," she replied.

Enrique is a boy who was in her class last year at school. God bless Enrique. Truly. I told her that it was not a nice word and that she should not say that. I explained that Enrique's parents might be okay with using that word, but her daddy and I were absolutely not. Then she said, "What does it mean anyway?"

I am never sure what to do in situations like this. If I make too big a deal out of it, she will surely be tempted to say it again. Forbidden fruit, you know.

But, quite possibly, if I had not reacted the way I did, she might have never said it again since she didn't even know what it meant. What is a parent to do? This is just one of the tricky parts of parenting.

On the flip side, Zeke is the star of his early childhood intervention speech therapy. He has made so much progress in the two and a half years he has been in the program. I cannot encourage parents enough to get early help if you suspect that something is not right. Many times parents just don't want to face the facts, but it is such a gift to your child to investigate and deal with any delays early. Zeke's latest phrase from speech? "Mommy, I love you and I like you." and "I want to tuddle (cuddle) with you, Mommy."

These are words parents can never get enough of.

So, we take the good with the bad. Such is life. We can't wait for our kids to talk and then when they do, we just worry about what they will say next. If they are extroverts, we worry double. Michael smugly tells me this is true no matter *what* age the extrovert is. I thought about telling him that "introverts suck."

But I thought better of it.

22 A Poetic Mother's Day

T'was the day known as Mother's Day all over the world,
And I woke with great joy knowing I would be spoiled!

The cards from the children were made with such care
A magnet, photo bookmark, and affection to spare!

Morning worship was a blessing and lunch a real treat,
Macaroni Grill really can't be beat.

The children were nestled all snug in their beds
for a midday nap and some rest for their heads.

And Michael and I with our large Diet Cokes,
Had just settled down for TV and some jokes.

When back in Zeke's room there arose such a clatter
Michael leapt from the La-Z-Boy to see what was the matter!

I heard him gasp and then cry "Oh, Zeke!"
Curiosity filled me—I knew I must peek.

I crept round the corner when I heard bathwater run,
I should have known better than to think it was fun.

When what to my horror-filled eyes should appear?
Zeke's room covered in poop—and him grinning ear to ear.

Michael scrubbed Zeke and I scrubbed the floor,
And all this on Mother's Day—what a dreadful chore!

There was poop on the bed, and poop on the floor,
Poop on the table and poop on the door.

Poop on books, on toys, and on walls,
It looked like a vacation to Poop-Agra Falls!

Oh yes, my dear friends, this much is true:
Toddlers in Pull-Ups are a danger to you.

But once things were clean and some time had gone by,
By my children's rooms I walked, and what did I spy?

Julia's beautiful face resting in complete peace,
Zeke, blissfully unaware of the extra elbow grease.

Blessings from God, no doubt in my mind
A happier mother you'd look hard to find.

And as the day came to a less stressful end,
I settled down to rest with my very best friend.

And he heard me whisper in a voice filled with love,
"Thank you so much, heavenly Father above."

23 My Greatest Gifts

Some days, life with children feels like a prison sentence. I am sorry to say it like that, but it is true. No one tells you that at your baby shower. It wouldn't look very poetic written across the cake! Plus, pregnant women are emotional enough as it is. But there are many other days that you wish you could freeze time—every year that Michael and I video the children running down the hallway to see what Santa has left— we get so few of those years.

At breakfast this morning, Julia asked to lead the prayer. We had just opened all of the presents from Santa and were sitting down to one of her favorite breakfast treats: iced orange rolls and strawberries. There were a million things she could have thanked God for. Her prayer took a different turn.

"Dear God, please be with all the children today who don't have presents. And help the ones who need a home. Amen."

Well, I could feel the tears welling up in my eyes as I expressed to her what a spiritually mature prayer that was.

She was quite pleased and smiled at me. "Are you going to put that on your blog?" she asked.

At lunch, with Nana and Papa present, she repeated the same, exact prayer. She said it word for word. This time, she prayed while squinting her eyes to see what everyone's reaction would be. She caught me looking at her. Not quite as spiritually mature. But—she is six! Oh, to have more years like this one.

We shared another funny moment as Julia was telling Zeke and me about her future plans.

"I want to start a day care program so that I can take care of all the children of the world who don't have a home. I will give them all food so that no child in the world is hungry. And then when I get fired from that job, I will open a store and sell underwear."

I am not making this up. How could I possibly be that creative?

And then there is our Zeke. Zeke told us many times today that Christmas is not about presents. It is about Jesus. He was very sweet tonight when I tucked him in. As I rubbed my hand across his little, blonde forehead, I wanted once again to freeze time.

"You are my little baby and I love you so much, Zeke," I said.

He pulled away from my hand indignantly. "Mommy, I am not a baby. I am a big boy."

"You are a big boy. But you will always be my baby," I explained.

And so he will. And so will Julia. What a beautiful day. And how very thankful I am for these, my greatest gifts.

24 Snapshots of Daddy

The house is quiet right now. This is a rare thing indeed, since both children rarely nap at the same time any more. Even Michael is snoozing on the couch—a rare treat for him on this Father's Day.

I am sitting in Zeke's room, watching his fingers twitching in his sleep. His eyelids are fluttering as he breathes in and out peacefully. He will be waking soon. Sweet moments. These are the snapshots that linger in the memory.

My mind reflects on my own childhood snapshots, specifically today the ones that include my daddy. I remember:

Riding on my daddy's back.

The sound of his coming in through the backdoor every day, without fail, at five o'clock.

Family dinner, every night.

Prayer time in my bed.

Hearing him read to me from *The Velveteen Rabbit* & *Aesop's Fables.*

Leg massages in the evening when I had "growing pains."

Waking to the sound of daddy praying beside my bed when I was very sick.

Waiting in the laundry room for the occasional spanking.

Knowing that it really, truly did hurt my dad more than it hurt me.

Riding with my dad in the car as we brought a homeless man to our house for Thanksgiving.

Visiting Dad's office at the print shop in Decatur, Alabama, and my daddy buying me Bugles from the vending machine.

Seeing him kiss my momma in the kitchen every night.

Dates to McDonald's for sausage biscuits with grape jelly.

Telling my dad at age twelve that I was too big for him to spank.

Finding out I was wrong about that.

Family meeting and prayer when Dad was out of work.

Daddy telling me that my cousin had been killed in a motorcycle accident.

Long talks about heaven.

Learning to drive a stick shift.

"Act as pretty as you look."

Knowing he was waiting up for me to get home, even if he was asleep on the couch.

My dad's forgiveness and mercy when I disappointed him deeply.

Hearing my daddy tell my ex-boyfriend who was mistreating me, "You leave Melanie alone or I will have to come to Abilene and take care of it myself."

Walking me down the aisle.

"Michael, you may now kiss my daughter."

Crying with me after miscarriage.

Seeing my daddy praying through the neonatal intensive care window when Julia was born with thyroid problems.

Incredible faith even through a Parkinson's diagnosis.

Hearing my dad speak at our church, and reflecting on what an amazing story he has to share about the faithfulness of God.

Watching him play the piano while my own kids dance.

Funny thing about life, these snapshots are as vivid to me today as when the moments occurred. Yet, none of them seemed particularly momentous at the time. When the kids were very little, I would get frustrated with myself as a mother. Usually it was because something I planned didn't turn out exactly how I thought it should have. Having the perfectionist gene, I would imagine the outcome of my planning and efforts, only to be disappointed when the picture at the end did not match the one in my imagination. Sometimes I would get frustrated with myself because I lost my temper and spoke harshly. I still struggle with that one. Michael wisely reminds me that raising children is a marathon, not a sprint. Trust and love are not built on big, momentous occasions, but on layers of moments. Life is made from layers of moments. Like the ones we have before us right now.

So I celebrate my own father today. And I celebrate my children's father. And I celebrate the little moments of life, the snapshots that will one day become a memory.

The room is still quiet and my heart is full, as my eyes are drawn once again to my angel boy. He will surely be waking any moment. Quietly, I rise from the rocking chair and curl up beside him in the bed. And gently wrapping my arms around his body, I rest my head on his pillow, and watch him breathe.

"Melanie and the Terrible, Horrible, No Good Night"

I had just returned from our church's annual women's retreat. I preface this chapter with that information, because gals will understand the implication of that—I was exhausted. Women's retreat = eating too much candy, laughing, staying up late, and sleeping not nearly enough.

My husband left for a business trip once I returned from the weekend, and I eagerly awaited bedtime when I could stretch out with the whole bed to myself and get a great night of sleep. It was going to be wonderful!

Boy was I wrong. I was in for a terrible, horrible, no good night.

First of all, I am not usually a scaredy-cat. But, there had been a lot of talk at the women's retreat about spiritual warfare, and so I got myself all worked up. To make matters worse, against my better judgment I sat watching TV shows about haunted places and psychic children in America for the two hours preceding bedtime. Did you know there are actually lighthouses that are haunted? There are also psychic children who apparently can talk to dead people. I also learned that psychic children are incredibly creepy. I know. I know. I should have stayed away from shows like these. It is here that my saga begins.

It was ten o'clock when I turned off the TV. I brushed my teeth and washed my face, one half at a time, so that I didn't have both eyes closed at the same time. I quickly turned off the light and made it into bed in one, large leap, so that I didn't have to walk too many steps in the dark room. The house was very quiet and still. It was only about five minutes later when I started hearing noises in the attic. Right away I knew what it was. No, not the water heater or the air-conditioning unit. That would be far too rational an assumption.

Of course, it had to be the devil.

I have no earthly idea what the devil might be doing hanging out in my attic. But, I was convinced that he was waiting for me to close my eyes so he could attack me. The television show about psychic children had warned me that this might happen. I had opened a portal for the devil. Why, oh why, did I ever watch that show? Lucky for me, I have also watched lots of shows about exorcisms, so I knew exactly what to do. I prayed, using Jesus' name as many times as I could while still making sense. I sang a hymn all the way through, complete with the "Amen." Then I forced myself to close my eyes, first for only a few seconds (as a test, you know), and then longer with each attempt. Finally, I drifted off to sleep.

About a half hour later, I was jolted awake by the telephone ringing. Our answering machine was too loud and my own voice jarred me awake. The message that was recorded was a strange combination of noises and thirty seconds of someone pushing buttons on the phone. Very strange. Of course, this only served to freak me out more. Maybe the devil was making the call from another location to scare me. On the positive side, I was relieved that he was perhaps gone from the attic.

I went back to sleep, only to be jolted awake at five minutes after midnight by the strong sense that someone was standing inches from my face. Happily, it was not the devil. It was only Julia, who was having problems because of some itching on her feet. She had scratched them until they were bleeding and now was crying that she needed me to fix them. I stumbled out of bed, rummaged through the medicine basket to find antibiotic cream and went about my work as a horribly underpaid physician. She was content with my efforts and went quickly back to sleep.

I returned to my bed. The attic made a thump again.

I was awakened this time by the sound of Zeke's screams. I bolted up out of the bed and charged into his room to find him crying hysterically after waking from a bad dream. I resettled him, comforted him with a prayer (I was really good at praying at this point) and checked the thermostat. The air was too still and it was getting warm in his room. After bumping down the temperature a couple of degrees, I returned to my bed. But not for long.

I had just drifted back to sleep when Zeke screamed out again. The clock said two-forty-two. This time he had no explanation. I guess he just felt like screaming. At this point, I did too, but held back the impulse.

It took a little longer this time to clear my mind and relax. Being awakened by a child in distress leaves you in a hypervigilant state. So I lay there in the bed for a while, on pins and needles, hoping for no more screams and anticipating them at the same time. Sweet relief came as everyone was quiet. I considered closing my door at this point, but didn't want to miss hearing something important, so the door stayed open. Once again, I went back to sleep.

Zeke was up before the roosters. It was five o'clock when I heard his voice, beckoning his sister to wake up. Although the sun was not yet up, he was wide awake and assumed it was time to party. I kindly asked him to go back to bed. I pleaded with him just to play quietly in his room. I commanded him to be quiet. We had at least a ten minute verbal struggle which resulted in multiple threats on my part. What can I say? You cannot make someone go to sleep. Although at this point, I would have welcomed the ultimatum! I seriously considered going to the garage and sleeping in my car. I even contemplated going upstairs and sleeping in the attic with the devil. But I decided against it. Better to stick with the devil you know, right?

After approximately forty-five additional minutes of sleep, my alarm went off. I knew it was going to be a Starbucks kind of morning.

It was a terrible, horrible, no good night. But my mother says they have those— even in Australia.

26 Stitches

I never had to have stitches as a child. I should have had stitches, but I did not.

I spent my early childhood years in rural Alabama. It was a wonderful place to live, as we had a giant yard, complete with fruit trees, a fenced-in pasture behind our house, and a large drainage ditch that my brother and I affectionately called "the creek." On the left side of our property was a large dirt pile. I am sure that my parents did not care for the dirt pile, but to my brother and me, it was our own personal mountain. One day we noticed that there was a ladder leaned up against the mountain. So, of course, we assessed the potential danger and left it alone. Right. We had to climb it! Sadly, that did not go so well, as I slipped and cut my leg open on an exposed nail. I remember well what followed. As I sat on the bathroom counter, I could hear my parents' muffled whispers outside the bathroom door. I heard pieces . . . "do you think? . . . hospital? . . . stitches?" Keep in mind, I was already a child prone to dramatics. Well, those fragmented sentences sent me over the top. And I began my protest.

"Noooooo. I don't waaaaaant to go to the hospital!!! *Please* don't take me!!" This was followed up by several "Please! Please! Please!" in a row (always effective).

Mom and Dad talked about it privately and called a doctor, who apparently told them they could just use a special kind of bandage at home. The decision was made. No stitches. As I got older, I wished I had not protested, as I hated the scar that remains on my leg. But at the time, I was relieved.

My parents seemed relieved too, to be spared the drama that stitches would inevitably bring.

Now I understand why.

Zeke's mishap did not occur on a ladder leaned up against a dirt pile. It happened at Vacation Bible School. Didn't know that was dangerous? Me either.

It seems that during the free play time, Zeke took a pretty good fall in the gym in just such a way as to cookie cutter his eyebrow line with his glasses frames. I must say, I handled myself very well. I was like the poster child for moms in a traumatic situation. Zeke was brought to me by one of the helpers, blood streaming down his face, bloody glasses set on the table, blood drops on his shirt . . . he looked like he'd lost a cage fight. I stayed completely calm so as not to freak him out.

"Oh buddy, let's get your face cleaned off," I said, while inside screaming, "What in the *name of heaven* happened?" I cleaned and bandaged him and we finished VBS and the celebration lunch (I am the VBS director)—then headed to Michael's office where he confirmed what I already suspected—Zeke needed stitches. My husband knew this because he had many visits to the hospital as a little boy. Apparently, his "Please! Please! Please!" was not as effective as mine. He probably could have performed the procedure himself. Thankfully, that was not required.

Michael was able to leave work early, so we all took a family trip to the ER. The kids sang VBS songs all the way. Julia reminded Zeke that "Jesus gives us the power to be brave!" (Thank you, VBS!) She made him an "encouragement balloon" with stickers of the characters from the week. They laughed and sang. It was not your usual trip to the emergency room.

Once we got there, the staff took us back pretty quickly. The good news was—they no longer have to give children a shot first to numb the area. The process was actually very interesting. They have a gel now that deadens the area so a needle is not required, at least not at that point.

When it was time, Julia ran into the bathroom crying. Actually, we sent her into the bathroom because she sounded like she was at the Wailing Wall.

Julia: "My poor brother. Oh, my poor brother! Oh, Zeke. Oh. Oh. Oh."

Zeke did not cry.

Please tell me, however, how we can be in such an advanced day and age, and yet there is nothing better that can be used to administer stitches. It seriously looks like a fish hook. They jammed it through his brow again and again and again. Bless! I was so thankful he could not feel it. And that Michael and I are not queasy by nature. He did feel the pressure, though, and every once in a while uttered from under his wrappings (strait-jacket) "Ouch . . . dat urt me." But he made it through fine. And Julia did too, even though later she explained that she felt "very ignored." Good grief.

After approximately fifteen minutes of conversation about ice cream, we were finished. Then we went to get some real ice cream with Nana and Papaw.

Six months later . . .

Zeke had to get stitches. Again. This time was a lot harder, because Zeke is older and ready to rumble. He doesn't like to be messed with. To make things more difficult, it has only been months since the last incident, so he remembered exactly what was going to happen.

I stayed home with Julia, who had Kung Fu on Wednesday night, and Michael handled the ER visit alone. The nurse remembered us (Zeke is pretty cute and memorable, even with a bloody head) and she asked Michael, "Didn't Mom want to come?" Truth is, I did. I was sad that I couldn't be there in his moment of need. But, Michael is a great dad . . . he had it under control. The procedure went fine and thankfully, Zeke mostly remembered that stitches = ice cream.

Two days later . . . Friday morning was the day to take his hospital bandages off his head. According to the aftercare paperwork we were given, this sounded very simple. "After 24 hours, remove the bandage. Wash the area and use hydrogen peroxide to clean the wound. Apply a thin layer of Neosporin ointment. Reapply a bandage."

Easy, peasy, right?

Wrong! Ever tried to give a cat a pill? Think along those lines.

What they failed to acknowledge in the paperwork was that somehow, they managed to get gobs and gobs of his hair in the tape. They also used a very adhesive tape—waaaaayyyyy too adhesive. So, we came out of the gate struggling. Between each task, it looked more like this:

1. Chase Zeke around the house.
2. Wrestle him.
3. Sit on him while holding down his arms.

All this while making sure he didn't injure himself in the struggle. The whole time repeating the phrases, "Zeke, this is not going to hurt you" (it was), and "Zeke, I will give you a cookie" (we both got one). We had to repeat this process two times a day.

I lost track of how many cookies I had during that time.

If I had a time machine, I would go back to that day, when little Melanie Fudge was sitting on the bathroom counter. You might be thinking that I would advise my uncertain parents to go ahead with the stitches. After all, it would eliminate my future scar and leave me with a better sense that my parents were in charge.

Nope. I would look my parents straight in the eye and tell them, "Good call."

27 Road Trips and Ratings

Each July, I load up the kids and hit the road for Abilene to pick up our church's middle-school kids at Abilene Christian University Leadership Camp. This annual, two-day round trip has become very special for us all—we really look forward to it for several weeks beforehand. In fact, we rate our excitement throughout the trip on a scale of one to ten. My favorite picture of the children from the trip is of Zeke and Julia sitting on the steps to the hotel, freshly bathed after swimming at our hotel pool. Can you see it in your mind's eye? Ah, my pride and joy. They say that a picture paints a thousand words. Ha! This picture doesn't say *nearly* enough.

Wednesday night we were all loaded up and eager to leave the next morning. Both kids were reporting ratings of ten. I was even at a ten myself, or at least a strong nine. But Thursday proved to have its challenging moments.

Not pictured: Zeke popping out both of the lenses from his glasses "for fun." (PS—*not* fun.) There are no pictures of my searching through the entire rented Suburban, our luggage, the trash bag, and Zeke's socks. There are no pictures of Zeke's poor, bloodshot eyes the next day as he strained to see the DVD player for which we had paid extra. And, no picture of Michael's finally finding the lens, under the carpet, beside the bolt of the automobile floor on Saturday morning . . . once we had returned home (kid rating: eight, mom rating: two).

Not pictured: Mommy's asking nicely for Julia to get out of the pool for dinner time, Julia's procrastinating, Julia's getting lost on the way out of the pool and accidentally going back into the pool—multiple times. There are no pictures of Mommy's demanding that she exit the pool in a less-than-nice voice, or of Julia's screaming that I am "the meanest mommy in the world." Where was Zeke during all of this excitement? Well, also not pictured is Zeke, who spent the whole pool-exit battle time taking rolled up towels off the shelf and throwing them into the hot tub. And, unfortunately we don't have a picture of Mommy scooping eight towels out of the hot tub and dragging both children by their arms back to the elevator while strangers dialed Child Protective Service . . . or at least the front desk for a dry towel (kid rating: four, mom rating: one).

Not pictured: Zeke's dropping his entire cup of queso in his lap at dinner and Julia crawling on the floor to help clean it, only to wind up with most of it on her clothes, and a piece of queso-covered chip in her mouth. Yes, you read that right (mom rating: two, Zeke rating: eight, Julia rating: ten).

Not pictured: The kids' fun game from nine until ten of "let's change beds." There are no pictures of Mommy's threatening each child with a swat if they got up *one more time* only to be tested by Julia's losing a tooth and needing to come to the bathroom to spit. Zeke needed to go to the bathroom to watch her spit (kid rating: five, mom rating: minus one, tooth fairy rating: ten).

Not pictured: A *much* better Friday, complete with a tour of Abilene and Abilene Christian University with the kids, Julia's taking a real interest in my history and sharing hot chocolates at Starbuck's (All around: nine).

Not pictured: Julia's asking, Friday night back in her own bed, "Mommy, when do we get to go to Abilene again?" (kid rating: ten).

Not pictured: My own excitement for our next adventure together. (mom rating: ten, or at least a strong nine).

28 Hidden Treasure

Cleaning can be cathartic. Almost everyone will admit to that. Even a semi-pack rat like me will confess that cleaning out a closet or drawer can make me feel lighter, younger, more vivacious even. But, sometimes cleaning can be even more. This week I experienced that firsthand.

My mother was hospitable enough to host Zeke, our dog Zeus, and me on Monday, on the occasion when our air conditioning was out and we were waiting for the repair man, who will henceforth be referred to as *my hero*. Since Zeke was enjoying his afternoon nap, and Mom and Dad were going to be shifting around some furniture in the next couple of weeks, Mom and I decided to tackle the job of cleaning out her sewing desk.

We shared some light-hearted laughter as I encouraged (forced?) Mom to throw away multiple, aborted, needlepoint projects, two of her six decks of cards, and a giant ball of yarn scraps that she was convinced would be needed again in the future. But as we finished our second bag of trash, the treasures began to emerge, like my brother's *Return of the Jedi* members-only-style jacket, with patches from several great action movies from the 80s. There were shoe-laces from my junior high, brochures from our family's trip to Hawaii after Dad graduated from law school, cards from so many friends on the occasion of my birth, my actual birth announcement, and a correspondence course written forty years ago by Dad about the grace of God.

The last item we found was a small booklet from Mom's doctor entitled, *You Are Expecting!* Inside were menus intended to give expectant mothers maximum nutrition. My mother had carefully detailed her food journal, down to the spoonful—one cup of grapes, one half cup of cottage cheese . . . so many details documented. She had made notes inside the margin from her visit with the doctor. There was a list of items needed for the nursery which Mom had checked off with a pen as the items were obtained. She even kept a record of her weight at each doctor's visit.

You should know. My mom is a perfectionist. I could prove it in a court of law. I even have video proof. The day before Julia's first birthday, I asked my mom to come over and help me decorate her cake. After all, my mom is kind of an expert with birthday cakes. She made one for every one of my birthdays. My brother's too. I told her my general idea for how I wanted the cake to look. It would be like a big garden, with flowers of many colors scattered across the top and sides. The camera was rolling when we began discussing our project.

"Here we go!" I said, as I began piping out the first pink flower.

"Oh, don't you want to practice on some waxed paper first?" my mom cautioned.

"Practice on waxed paper? Ha!" I chuckled. "No, I was just thinking we would let the flowers fall how they fall."

This has always been my nature. It works for me. We are opposites in that way. Mom would have most definitely practiced first. I wonder how long it took her to make all of my birthday cakes . . .

Now as we looked through meticulous notes on her pregnancy, I could see her nature clearly reflected on the journal's pages.

"You really took this seriously!" I teased Mom.

Her eyes began to glisten with the beginning of tears.

"Well, yes . . . *of course* I did."

Of course she did. Mom always wanted to be a wife and mother. This was her most important task. As Charlotte from *Charlotte's Web* would say, this was her magnum opus. Her perfectionist nature, which sometimes frustrates and confounds me, was, in this case, a very good thing. God had perfectly equipped her for motherhood. Before she ever practiced icing a birthday cake, she had focused on getting this job done right. She wanted nothing more than for me to be a healthy baby. And she was going to do everything in her power to make it so. Now I saw my mom's quest for perfection in a different light.

It was motivated by love.

I was touched by this realization. Touched and humbled and honored. My mom had done all of this, for me. I saw her in a new light. And it was precious.

I don't think I will ever forget our afternoon cleaning out that desk. I will certainly never forget the treasure that I found there.

Temptation 29

This post is not about adultery. I have a very happy and fulfilling marriage and other times I just feel like being lazy. Regardless, I am not tempted in that way. This chapter is about a much more difficult temptation for me to resist. Of course, I am talking about baked goods.

I am doing Weight Watchers. This has been almost a year-long process, with another year before that of doing it on my own. After two years of purposeful eating, I am happy and proud to say, I have been pretty successful at it. Something about keeping track of my daily allowance of points jives well with my control-freak personality. What can I say?

Sometimes, though, the temptations are really hard to overcome. Lately, this tempting has come at me from the Starbucks scone. I am partial to the pumpkin variety, but the cranberry orange is really good, too. If you have never tried one—don't! One day I will probably travel to elementary schools giving presentations about saying no to scones. Actually, all baked goods for that matter. But I do know this: the Starbucks scone is a gateway pastry!

I have never considered myself an addict, but I imagine the struggle is similar. This was my inner conversation on the way to work yesterday:

"Wow, I *really* want a scone."
"I don't have enough points for a scone."
"I could eat soup for dinner and salad for lunch!"
"That's still not enough I bet."

"How many points *are* in a scone?"

"I could Google it."

"I can't Google it before I get to Starbucks though."

"I am *not* stopping to get a scone."

"Maybe just a nonfat latte."

"And a scone!"

"If I stop today, I will just want to stop tomorrow. No, no, no!"

"One day will *not* make that much difference."

"But I will feel so much better if I resist!"

Crazy-person, inner-voice exchange interrupted by Starbucks drive-through voice: "Welcome to Starbucks! What can I get started for you?"

Pause.

"A nonfat latte, please."

"Would you like any pastries with that?"

Longer pause.

"No, thank you."

(Inner voice): "but maybe next time . . ."

I have not been as successful on the home front. When you are working the Weight Watchers's program, it is a *bad* idea to be the cookie mom for your daughter's Girl Scout troop. It's not that the temptation is too great for me. So far, I have only eaten five cookies—in four days—but why put yourself through the torture?

The problem lies in the fact that there are extra boxes that are unaccounted for. Whatever is needed to fill out the large shipping box, the suppliers give us to sell. That means that I have eleven boxes of *unclaimed* Caramel Delights, ten boxes of *unclaimed* Peanut Butter Patties, and more. These sad, little unclaimed boxes call to me in the night.

"We are so sad and lonely. You're the cookie mom. You are supposed to love us! It's only $3.50 more . . . we're yuuuuuu-mmmmmy!"

This, on top of the gooey, buttery, heart-shaped Rice Krispie treats Julia and I made yesterday and both kids' school party stashes of assorted chocolates . . . it's almost too much to handle.

Twenty-one points just won't go that far! Maybe I can rework the numbers.

Our kids struggle with temptations too. For some it might be lying. For some it might be fighting. For Julia, it has been talking out in class. Her conduct grades indicate that this is definitely a weakness for her. She just has so much to say! And her wonderful thoughts and ideas must burst forth from her mouth and be shared with the world. Apparently, her teachers are not always in the mood for her unselfish and unending verbal gifts.

Recently, Julia's Papaw gave her a good suggestion.

"When you get to school, and you feel like talking out, just say a prayer and ask God to help you to have self-control," he encouraged.

Julia pondered the suggestion in a rare moment of silence.

"But, Papaw, I already know what I *should* do. I just don't really want to do it."

And there it is, folks. Out of the mouths of babes. In prayer, God has given us an escape hatch. We just have to be willing to open the door. And then we can resist temptation.

I can only pray that the escape hatch is not located near a Starbucks.

30 Family Camping (The Cold, Cold Night)

Growing up, I cannot remember ever going camping with my family. Although my mom is quite the gardener and my dad enjoys the beauty of nature, my parents are not big outdoor enthusiasts. Michael and I went with friends in our early years of marriage. We spent a ridiculous amount of money stocking up on all the equipment that we needed. Shortly after dinner on the first night, however, I became ill. I spent the night unzipping the tent . . . zipping the tent . . . unzipping the tent . . . zipping the tent. Putting on my shoes, hiking to the bathroom. Hiking back, taking off my shoes. Over and over again. Although I did get a lot of great exercise, I think I got a total of two hours of sleep. It was not a great experience.

Once the kids were of a reasonable age, we decided to try again. Family camping! It certainly sounded fun! We were not sure what to expect, but hoped for the best. I must say, we had a wonderful time being together without televisions, laptops—even without heat, though that was the hardest luxury to give up. The wind started picking up around the time the kids finally went to sleep. It was so strong, it blew the cover off our tent. We knew a weather change was on its way. Either that, or Mary Poppins was coming. We were right—about the weather change—not Mary Poppins. You see, a cold front came through in the middle of the night, and though we were prepared for a fifty-five degree night, we got a forty degree night. Brrr. That being said, the overall experience was wonderful.

Some of the highlights were:

Setting up the tent with Michael. I am always impressed by how well we work together when we need to. He is really quite good at putting things together.

Cooking hot dogs on the fire. Michael had the kids calling him Mr. Hot Dog Man. It was cute! Then they started calling me Bun Lady and we had to reel it in. I don't particularly want that one to stick.

S'mores. Enough said, right? If you are asking, "How many Weight Watchers's points are in a s'more?" the answer is, "Who cares?" I just enjoyed.

Singing "This Is the Day" around the fire. This was followed by a verse of "This Is the Night" and then "This Is the Morning," and then "This Is the Hot Dog Man."

The joy on Zeke's face when we told him he could pee on a tree.

The shock on Julia's face when Zeke did, in fact, pee on a tree.

Singing "How Great Thou Art" to the kids as a lullaby—while gazing at the stars above us through the net roof of the tent.

Looking up at those same stars with Michael beside the fire while listening to the kids giggling in the tent. It was one of those precious moments of complete peace and contentment.

The cold night coming to an end with lots of family cuddling at the break of dawn. Zeke's squeezing into my sleeping bag with me and holding my hand, without any prompting.

Driving home to warm baths and a heated house.

Knowing that this fun and precious family is mine to keep. What a blessing.

Will we ever invest in a camper or an RV? Probably not. I am more of an uptown girl than an earth mama. However, I am certain that we will do it again soon.

But next time, I think we will wait until summer.

31 Wake–Up Call

There are lots of ways to wake up in the morning.

When I was a little girl, I was difficult to wake up. My mom would start out with a really sweet voice.

"Sweet girl, it is time to get up." Think *Mary Poppins*.

This would morph into something a little less sweet as she made follow-up attempts at getting me out of the bed. Within several minutes, she resorted to "Get up!" Think *The Shining*.

The bright lights of my bedroom were turned on. Finally, she resorted to rubbing a cold washcloth on my face. All of this morning drama inevitably concluded with my huffing and puffing out of bed, angry at the mistreatment I had received, and my mom's wanting to run away to Mexico.

Eventually, my mom purchased an alarm clock for me. It had the *Sesame Street* logo and had Big Bird's voice on it. I will never forget it, probably because it repeated the same sentences over and over again.

"Hello, it's me, Big Bird, and it's time to get up! Open your little eyes now. Don't roll over and go back to sleep. C'mon now, one foot out of bed, now the other one. Okay, have a nice day. And don't forget to wind the clock."

I must have heard it five thousand times. Everyone in the house heard it five thousand times. My poor family. No wonder my little brother hated Big Bird.

Of course, there is the traditional "wake-up call" that you can request from the hotel lobby personnel. This used to be done by a real, live person. I imagine they got tired of the abuse. Now when you finally drag your body to the telephone, it is usually a recorded message or just music playing in the background.

Yes, there are lots of ways to wake up. Some are nicer than others.

"Mom! I need you to come wipe my bottom!"

My day began with those poetic words. When I didn't come running (shock!) Zeke made it more specific, "Mom! I went poop and I need you to wipe the poop off my bottom!"

Sigh.

And with that bit of childhood prose, I was up. Motherhood is so romantic.

At breakfast, the kids and I discussed our future plans. They wanted to know when they would be old enough to get married. I explained to them that there is not a specific age for getting married, so anytime (after college graduation) would be perfectly acceptable. They both seemed content with this answer. Zeke wanted to discuss the subject a little more thoroughly. He wanted to know why he couldn't marry Julia.

"Don't worry," I assured him. "When you are old enough to get married, you won't *want* to marry Julia." He looked unsure, but seemed to take my word for it.

Julia informed me that she was planning to make Zeke her roommate in college. Zeke countered that he was not going to go to college. He wants to stay home and live with me.

I had a horrific flash-forward to my grown son yelling down the hall, "Mom, I need you to . . ." Well, you know.

Our kids have always been early risers. No matter what time they are down for the night, their little internal clocks always wake them around six-thirty. Bless their hearts. It was harder when they were younger. These days Julia is starting to sleep in a little more. There are some school days when I actually have to wake her up. I start out sweetly, just like my mom did. I have only had to use the cold washcloth once so far.

Maybe I will dig out that *Sesame Street* alarm clock.

Then again . . .

32 Grace and the Babysitter

It was Jamie's first time to babysit for us. We typically use my mother as our sitter, and when she is not available, we have a couple of teens that live in the neighborhood who can watch the kids. On this particular day, my parents were out of town and we had no luck finding any of our other regulars, so we thought we would try someone new. Jamie was a very intelligent teenager. She had always struck us as very responsible and mature for her age. So I gave her a call.

"Great news!" I reported to Michael that afternoon. "I got her!"

We both rejoiced at the news and began to make our plans for the evening. There was a movie at the Alamo Drafthouse Cinema that we were interested in seeing and we looked forward to a nice evening out together.

When Jamie arrived at the house, I began to go through the kids' routine with her. To make things easier, I had already bathed them and put them in their pajamas. It was six and Zeke would be put to bed at seven-fifteen and Julia at seven-forty-five. Piece of cake. I left our emergency numbers on the counter, we said our goodbyes to the kids, and out the door we went.

We were about halfway through the movie and were still finishing our meal when my cell phone began vibrating in my lap. Glancing at the caller ID, I recognized the cell phone number immediately. It was a close friend from our neighborhood.

"Hello?" I whispered, as I tried to make my way out of the theater without annoying everyone around me.

"Melanie, we need you to come home."

Instantly, my blood turned to ice. I felt sick.

My neighbor continued, "The kids are okay, but Jamie and Julia are locked out of the house."

"Where is Zeke?" I asked in a panic. He was still very young. I imagined him walking around the house alone, crying and scared.

"He's okay," my neighbor continued. "I am looking in his window right now and he is asleep in his bed. But we need you to come now and let them in."

I returned to the theatre and through whispers broke the news to Michael that he would not be finishing his six-dollar drink and that we would possibly never know if the heroine took back her cheating boyfriend. Knowing that we could not wait for change, we left a pile of money for our server and began walking quickly to the car.

"What happened?" Michael asked in frustration.

"I have no idea." I answered, my blood still feeling like slush in my veins. Knowing that the kids were all right, my fear began to turn to curiosity, and anger.

The drive home was a tense one, as Michael and I have different ways of dealing with these kinds of situations. As usual, I began to empathize with the underdog. As usual, Michael was not so full of understanding.

"She must have been very scared," I reasoned.

"Well, whatever you do, don't tell her that 'it's okay,' because it isn't." he retorted.

As we pulled up to the house, it looked like something from the set of *Cops*. The neighbors were standing outside on the driveway. Beside them was Jamie, looking as if she had been through a war. Beside Jamie was Julia, in her nightgown and tennis shoes. She actually looked quite excited.

Then we listened as the story was told.

Zeke had been put to bed at seven-fifteen, just as we had instructed. Apparently, after he was down, Julia told Jamie that she "usually likes to take a walk before bed." Never mind that the child was already in her nightgown. Never mind that Zeke was already in bed. For some reason unknown to me, Jamie believed her. So, they put on their tennis shoes and left Zeke alone while they went to take a walk around the block. Although neither of them remembered doing it, the door was locked when they came back home. Since it was going to be only a short walk, Jamie had left her cell phone inside our house.

This is when the horror began.

Jamie started crying. Julia took charge and began to brainstorm solutions. She knew that we had a loose board in the fence, and suggested that they both try to squeeze through the opening. Maybe the back door would be unlocked. It was not. They tried all the windows. They were locked. They considered breaking a window, but decided against it. And so began the tour of the neighborhood.

First they went to our next door neighbor's house. The neighbors were not home. Then the girls tried a couple of other houses nearby with the same result. Jamie was aware that their options were becoming limited and her sense of anxiety was growing at this point. Still believing that she knew the solution, Julia took Jamie to another neighbor's house farther down the street, insisting that she knew the people who lived there. She did not. She thought it was the home of a nice lady that she had seen before. It was not. A man in an undershirt answered the door to discover our crying babysitter, and my young daughter in her nightgown.

"Can you take us down the street to our friends' house?" Julia asked the stranger.

The man agreed to give them a ride. So Jamie and Julia climbed into the strange man's pickup truck and headed down the road.

It was at this point in the story that I began to feel my blood heating up again. The bad judgment of our supposedly responsible sitter was almost too much for me to handle. Michael had heard enough, so he went inside at this point to check on Zeke.

Jamie completed the story by telling me that our friends had answered the door, brought the girls inside their home, thanked the man in the pickup truck, sent him back home, and then called us. End of story.

She began to cry again. "I am just so sorry," she said through her tears.

I wanted to speak harshly to her. After all, I would *never* have done something like this when I was a young babysitter! It was at that moment, I had a flashback to another day, long ago but not forgotten.

I was sixteen years old. I worked at a daycare center near our home. Typically I worked the after-school shift, from three to six, but since it was spring break week, the director of the center had agreed to give me some more hours. I had stayed up much too late the night before, so when it was time for the two-year-olds to have their rest time, I decided to take advantage of the silence and close my eyes for just a moment, too. It didn't take too long before my miniature chair became uncomfortable. In the corner of the room, I spied a mattress on the floor in a play-house area. That would be the perfect place to relocate my rest, I decided.

I don't remember falling asleep. But suddenly I heard a voice calling my name.

"Melanie!"

"Melanie!"

"Melanie! Wake up!"

It was not God, although pretty quickly I wished it had been. It was the director of the daycare. Coming to my senses, I could see that the lights had been turned on. Too much time had passed. There were two-year-olds wandering around the room. Some were still sleeping on their mats. One chubby girl was helping herself to graham crackers while a little boy was playing in glue at a table. To make matters worse, parents had started coming to pick up their children. And there I was, spread eagle on the mattress, slobbering and snoring.

"I am just so sorry." I heard those words again. This time I could not tell if they had come from Jamie or from my own memory. It was almost as if our stories had fused together.

I reached out my arms to Jamie and brought her into an embrace. "I know you were scared. You did what you thought was best," I said.

The daycare director did not fire me. She showed me grace. But she did put me back on the after-school shift. I never taught the two-year olds in class again. And we would not ask Jamie to babysit again, although we did still pay her for her time that night. It felt like a very long night.

I swallowed. "We all make mistakes, Jamie. I forgive you." I could feel her exhale within our embrace.

And I think a part of me did, too.

Bless Your Heart

33

I was born in the deep South. Alabama, to be precise. When someone gets on your very last fiber of nerve in the South, you don't react in a typical fashion. There is no yelling and rarely even direct confrontation. You just bless their heart. It goes something like this,

"Well, that store clerk *must* be new because she didn't give me my receipt, bless her heart."

"And she was wearing too much perfume, bless her heart."

"And, I don't mean to be rude, but she certainly got hit with the ugly stick . . . bless her heart."

Just a little Southern trivia for you, in case you didn't know that.

When you are a mom . . . specifically, a mom of a boy . . . there are "those days." Well, this was one of those. Zeke was on a roll today.

It started when Zeke found a crayon in the back seat of my car this morning. Why in heaven's name there was a crayon in the back seat, I am sure I don't know. You see, I know better than that. Well, actually, there were two—a blue one and a red one. Zeke chose red and illustrated his favorite daydreams on the inside car door. Julia (my nearly seven-year-old who should know better) thought this was a fun opportunity to show off her art skills and chose the blue crayon to make pretty stars on her side of the car door. So far, it has not come off—on either side.

Later in the day we went to Gymboree for a quick shopping trip. Did you know that most of the racks of clothes at Gymboree are on rollers? They are. They are incredibly mobile. Little known fact, you can roll them all around the store. You can roll them until everyone in the store is looking at you—but trust me, mostly they are looking at your mother.

This evening I was putting away the Gymboree clothes, which took me several minutes. I came through the kitchen because I heard a strange noise. Turns out, the noise I heard was the sound that the kitchen sink spray attachment makes when it is spraying water at high speed. By the way, who on earth thought that inventing that gizmo was a good idea? Does anyone out there really spray their dishes with that thing? The collateral damage is just too great. Back to Zeke. He had pulled a chair up to the sink and was helping Julia clean her Baby Alive plate when he discovered that he could spray water throughout the kitchen and living room. The kitchen floor was soaked. The living room carpet was soaked. The couch was wet, too. The piano, the mirror behind the piano, the kitchen counter, DVD movies (including a couple of Netflix that don't belong to us), the medicine basket . . . all got a washing. And Zeke got a spanking.

It's just a day in the life of my son, people.

Bless his heart.

Regrets

34

I have had moments of regret in my life. Everyone has. The ability to choose our own actions and words makes regret an inevitability. But one thing is for certain, regret feels rotten.

As I write this, I have regrets.

Julia and I had a rough time of it this morning. It seems that the older she gets, the more complicated it is being in relationship with her. Those reading who have teens right now, or those who have had teens, particularly girls, are probably laughing right now. Or crying. I know my mom did a lot of that during my teen years!

Julia is not a teen. She is almost seven. But our relationship dynamic is already complicated. She is moody. And if I am honest, I am moody too. Two moody women in one room . . . is one too many. Michael would insert that it is actually *two* too many. Regardless.

In addition to being moody, Julia is indecisive, but very opinionated. Trust me when I tell you, you can be both. And the combination is vicious, because these particular traits mean that you don't know what to do but don't like anyone else's suggestions either. Julia is especially prone to these behaviors when it comes to choosing her clothes. And, I don't mind helping my children dress, but I hate wasting my time. Clothes were the problem on this particular morning.

I had asked Julia to go and get dressed. She replied that she would appreciate some help, because she didn't know what to wear. I happily agreed to assist her and put together a very cute outfit for her: black pants with blue, red, and green polka dots, a black shirt and her blue faux-fur vest. It was precious. I was proud. She looked like she had stepped out of a cute children's magazine. Julia was not impressed.

"Mom, this is not good. I just want to wear my jeans."

Mind you, there was no mention of the jeans whatsoever prior to this moment. I had a feeling that if I would have suggested the jeans she would have picked the polka-dotted pants. But, I agreed that it was okay by me if she wanted to change into jeans. That would at least still go with the rest of the outfit. She came out five minutes later in the black shirt paired with a navy skirt. It was not a terrific look, in my opinion, especially in comparison to the ensemble that I had presented, but in the name of fostering independence, I kept my mouth shut.

Just as we had cleared that hurdle, she launched into a fit about her socks being tight, and how much she hates *all* her socks and especially the *stupid* ones and how she needs new shoes and hates her mean, mean teacher. Furthermore, she hates school and wishes she could go and cut the dumb school in half with scissors.

All this before eight or even my cup of coffee.

I presented Julia with two different pairs of socks, neither of which were to her liking. One was too plain. The other was too decorated. She couldn't find her shoes. This is PE day, so we *had* to find the tennis shoes. She discovered a small lump of gum in her hair, which I had to brush out. She dilly-dallied around when it was time to brush her teeth.

All of this excitement put us in the drop-off carpool lane at two minutes until the tardy bell. I am certain that she ended up being late.

"Mom, am I going to be tardy? I have never been tardy before. Will I get in trouble?"

I didn't try to alleviate her fears. I was frazzled and angry, so instead I launched into a speech: "We don't have time for multiple costume changes in the morning. You will have to go to the office and explain why you are late! You can tell them that you just couldn't get it together."

I should have told her that everyone is late sometimes. But I didn't. I should have hugged and kissed her goodbye for the day. But I didn't. I should have told her that her clothes didn't matter. But it bugged me that she had changed. I did manage to get our daily prayer in before she left the car, but it was rushed and strained. We had both had it.

As I watched my little girl dressed in her black and navy walking into the school, her face reflected the morning. She didn't look mad anymore. Her face just looked sad. And then she disappeared into the building where she will spend her day.

And I have regrets.

35 The Move

Today was a memorable day in Julia's life. It was one of those days that you remember forever. This was the day that Julia's best friend moved away.

We have been talking about the move for several weeks. I had done my best to prepare her. She knew the day was coming. But on the way to her friend's house after school, Julia began to get choked up.

"Mommy, this is horrible," she said.

I tried to coach her as best I could. "It's going to be okay, J. Just make sure that you tell her what you want to say. This is your opportunity to say what you need to say."

Watching the girls together was almost like watching a documentary on exotic animals. Children's ways are very different from adult ways. They joined hands. They smiled at each other. Then they ran. They ran around a neighbor's tree laughing. They were silly. For several minutes there was only the sharing of joy, with minimal words. And then the time came to say goodbye.

Julia hugged her friend, whom she has known and loved for five years.

"I am really going to miss you," Julia said, as clearly and maturely as an adult.

Flashing through my mind was a slide show of the past: the birthday parties, trips to the pumpkin patch, visits when siblings were born, carpool rides, Valentine celebrations, sleepovers, finger painting. I saw the girls running through the house dressed as princesses and fairies. And then we were back, standing in the driveway by the tree. Saying what needed to be said.

"You have been a great friend."

"You have, too."

"I love you."

"I love you too."

It has been almost thirty years since my own childhood move. I can still remember when my parents announced that we would be packing up and heading to Texas. My dad had a wonderful job opportunity which he believed was from God's own hand and it was the best thing for our family. I wish I could say that my first thought was about the friends I would leave behind, but it would be a lie. I was worried that there would not be a McDonald's in Texas. False alarm on that one. Turns out they are everywhere (for anyone else who may have that concern). My second thought was for my friends. I remember heading into the classroom on the last day of school, armed with a small piece of paper that held my new address. I remember that I spelled Katy, C-a-d-d-y. I thought all my classmates would write me. We would be pen pals! They did not. Or maybe they did and the mail just went to the booming metropolis of Caddy, Texas. I don't know which.

Saying goodbye to my best friend Ashley, was the hardest part. My mom had driven me to her house to say our farewells. Even as children, we felt the gravity of the situation, yet we were unsure of how to handle the big emotions that we were feeling. So we traded treasures. I gave her a stuffed animal to remember me by. She gave me a Holly Hobby mirror and comb combo. We hugged. And we said goodbye.

And now my own daughter was having her own experience with goodbye. As we pulled away from the house, the tears came. Sobs, actually.

"Mommy, this is just horrible," she repeated from earlier.

And I felt the sadness too. For myself and for my little, heartbroken girl.

So, we turned off the Elmo CD that I had put in for distraction and we both gave in to the tears. I held her hand and we both cried. This time I didn't try to talk her out of her tears. In that moment, it didn't matter that there was a generation between us. In that moment, I was a little girl again too. We cried together as peers.

Certainly, we will stay in touch with our friends. We will send cards and exchange e-mails. But today will linger in our memories.

We will always remember the move.

Confessions of
a Parenting Failure

Hello, my name is Melanie. And I am doing a wretchedly horrible job being consistent in disciplining my three-year-old son. (You say, "Hello, Melanie.")

Zeke has been acting out. He is into mischief daily. This is normal for a child his age. Julia went through this stage too. Michael and I were a team in her early years. We were consistent. Firm, but loving. With Julia, the law is the law. When she needs correction, it is easy for me to step up and do what must be done. Even when her bad choice is funny, I can usually do the right thing and hold in my giggles by biting my cheek a little. And she is growing up beautifully. Now it is Zeke's turn to test his boundaries. Trouble is—I am not consistent with him. I am a pushover. I am easy. I am loosey-goosey. I am "coo-coo for cocoa puffs" with Zeke.

"Mama, I picked dis fwower for *you*," Zeke said this morning, handing me a dandelion from the yard.

Isn't that *cute*? This is just one of the cute things that Zeke is doing these days and part of the reason I cannot seem to get on board with disciplining him. He can be such a stinker, people! As my friend Julie used to say, "The mayor of Rascalville." But, he is *so cute*. Did I already say that?

Part of this is because he is my baby. He is also my boy. There is some kind of special magic between a mommy and her boy. In addition, he had a rough beginning, being in multiple therapies his first couple of years of life.

He still has speech and motor delays which make him seem younger than he truly is. We spent several days and nights together following his eye surgery, as he required almost constant supervision during those first days post-op. Beside all of that, he is also my only cuddly baby. Julia was never a big cuddler. She is too independent. She would tolerate the closeness for about three minutes before saying,

"Mommy. Would you please put me down?"

Not Zeke.

"Mommy, I want to tuddle wif you." Goo, goo, gah, gah. I am smitten.

And so, I continue to giggle to myself when he misbehaves, bring him into the bed with me in the morning before the approved time of seven (at least I *tell* him it is seven; what he doesn't know won't hurt him!), and I hang back when he needs correcting so that maybe Daddy will do it.

I know this is all wrong. I hear Jiminy Cricket telling me to let my conscience be my guide. I see the little SuperNanny on my shoulder crying. But, I really don't see the harm. There is no reason to believe he cannot still grow up to be a law-abiding citizen. Right?

At least in Rascalville.

Bye-Bye Baby

37

This morning the very last piece of "baby" left our house. We have slowly said goodbye to the baby paraphernalia for the past year or so—little bits at a time. The clothes were the first to go as they were outgrown, then the crib, the toys, the baby monitor. A couple of weeks ago some friends of ours came for the baby mattress and the rocking chair. We were happy to see it passed along to people we love. It was a little sad, but mostly a celebration of the stage that we have made it through!

For some reason though, this morning was hard.

When I walked outside with the last bag of garbage for this morning's pickup, I saw that Michael had put the stroller beside the can. The stroller. Our last piece of baby.

This stroller and I have been friends a long time. Longer than some people stay married! I still remember when Michael and I got it. I still remember my first trip around the block pushing it. It was one of those mornings when baby Julia would not stop crying, despite my best efforts to comfort her. My emotions were frazzled from postpartum blues and cabin fever was beginning to set in. "Why don't you take her in the stroller and just walk around the block?" my wise mother suggested. And so Julia and I did. We walked. And it worked. The fresh air and exercise energized me. The change of scenery calmed her. We found a common ground that brought us peace. I think we walked for an hour that day. It was the first of many walks. The bumpy tread on the wheels was smooth by the time Julia reached her first birthday.

Then came baby Zeke. I remember many more walks with Zeke. Because his walking came a little later, he had more opportunities to enjoy that stroller. The stroller participated in three Thanksgiving Day family-fun runs. The stroller has been on trips with us—to Dallas, to Abilene, to Tennessee, to Georgia. It has been in countless malls and parks. It has been pulled out of multiple car trunks and ridden on several airplanes. I also remember the days when both kids learned how to climb out of the stroller, and I remember chasing them around stores to get them back in it.

As we were leaving this morning for school, a red pickup truck pulled up. "Are you throwing away that stroller?" the man inside the truck inquired.

"The stroller?" I repeated, probably in an effort to buy myself one more moment of time.

I took in a breath.

"Yes, we are."

And we loaded it into the red truck. The driver waved and smiled as he drove away.

And then, with great resolve and joy for my future years of big kids, and with a little sadness, I said goodbye to baby.

The Gate

38

When our children were little, Michael and I put a gate in front of their doors. The gate served an important function: keeping them in their rooms, while still allowing us to see what was going on inside. When we started potty training Julia, the gate had to be retired. But not long after, we pulled it back into service with toddler Zeke.

We had great luck with the gate. Neither child ever tried to climb over or escape the gate. It just was a part of our life. Julia would even ask a babysitter to please remember to put up her gate.

I loved that gate.

Mostly because I knew that once I snapped it closed after tuck-in time, that was that. Until morning.

Those days are gone. Now that both children need the freedom to go to the bathroom when the need arises, their doors are always open. There is no guarantee that someone will not come wandering around the house in the night. This sometimes creeps me out, truth be told. Sometimes I have morbid thoughts of children taking out their frustrations on their sleeping parents.

I'll bet Lizzy Borden's parents wished they'd had a gate.

Last night I became especially aware of the gate's absence. My night could only be compared to that of Ebenezer Scrooge's infamous night from *A Christmas Carol*. The fun began around ten-thirty when I went to bed. I had a hard time dozing off, but managed to relax and sleep by eleven. I was awakened at eleven-thirty by the pitter-patter of little feet. Zeke came to tell me that he couldn't find his blanket. I walked him back to his room, where he turned on his light and immediately found his blanket. Could he have done this alone? Certainly. But, I wasn't mad. I just went back to bed.

At twelve-thirty I was awakened by the second visitor. Julia wandered into our room sniffing. Afraid that she was having a relapse of illness, I immediately snapped into awake mode.

"Are you okay?" I asked.

"I am scared of my room," she replied. This doesn't happen often, so I walked her back into her room, tucked her back in, and comforted her with a prayer and an extra light.

I went back to sleep, where I remained until one-thirty when I received my last visitor. Our dog, Zeus, had been up each of the other times with me and now believed it was morning, or at least close enough. He had to go out to potty. So outside I trekked.

I had another visit from Zeke at four-thirty, but just pulled him into the bed with me to avoid getting up again.

The comparison between the literary classic and my night ends there. You see, Ebenezer's night of visitors resulted in a better Ebenezer. My night only made me feel more like Scrooge.

Dear Gate, I miss you. Love always, Melanie.

Growing Up

Julia just celebrated her seventh birthday! It is incredible that seven years have gone by since she was born. I am amazed each day by her maturity, her creativity, her zest for life, her powerful spirit, her compassionate heart, her inner and outer beauty. She recently told me that she had a "crush" on a boy in her class. His name is Nicholas—he is a wonderful kid. I explained to her that I thought (and her daddy certainly concurs) that she is too young to have a crush, but that we were more than happy for her to have Nicholas as a friend. I asked her why she liked him, halfway expecting to hear the usual language of crushes: "he's cute" or something like that. She told me instead that it was because Nicholas was kind, and that he stands up for people who need help. You can't really beat that, folks. Hopefully, this quality will stay on her list of necessary characteristics as she grows up.

Zeke is nearly four years old. He has developed a charming habit of adding the words "poop" and "bad" to every song he sings. Sometimes he can get the words in multiple times during a song. For instance, at lunch today he serenaded me with this classic hit: "Twinkle, twinkle, little poop, how I wonder poop, poop, poop. Up above the bad world so high, like a bad poop in the sky . . . "

Like I said—charming. And we were worried that he wouldn't talk.

Most of the time the kids love playing together. They enjoy playing together in the backyard, coloring with chalk, swinging on the swing set. When it comes to sharing, especially Leapster cartridges, all bets are off. Zeke can be very persistent. He can say, "I want that cartridge" one hundred times in a minute. Julia sometimes gives in to him just to quiet him up. I understand this technique, since it is what got us in the middle-of-the-night-visits-to-cuddle-mommy-club. I am working myself out of a hole on that one.

The other morning Zeke came into my room and asked to cuddle. This was after a night of several visits and I was *so* over it. "Zeke, you have lost the chance to cuddle with me this morning, because you disturbed us in the night."

"Mommy, you are mean."

"Zeke, this is called discipline."

"If you love me, you will cuddle with me!" (Oh yes, he said it.)

"I do love you, Zeke, which is why I have to teach you to make good choices."

Sometimes I wonder who is teaching whom. This parenting stuff is hard work.

But now that I think about it, so is growing up. And I suppose we never stop doing that.

At the Movies

40

Going to a real movie at the theater is a big deal in our family. You might even call it a rite of passage. To give you some perspective, Julia's first movie was when she was six. We went to see *American Girl*. Zeke saw his first movie at age three. (Everything seems to come a little earlier with the second child, for better or for worse.) It was *Earth*, a rated-G, shortened version of the series *Planet Earth* that aired on the Discovery Channel last year. I assumed that the producers had tamed down the segments featuring animals chasing and eating other animals, which last year sent Julia screaming off to her room. We assured both kids it would be fun and that there would be no scary parts.

The excitement started as we found Theater One. Julia pulled back as we heard the loud preview music playing inside. Zeke saw her reaction and raised it by ten. He squealed in fear and took off running out of the theater, past the ticket booth, and into the mall area. Remember the scene in *The Wizard of Oz* when the wizard says, *"Go!"* and the cowardly lion bursts through the doors like his tail is on fire? It was like that.

I caught up with him, like a wolf chasing a deer, and once again reassured him that the movie was going to be fun. I picked him up and carried him (kicking and crying) back to Theater One, hoping that would be the case.

The movie was awesome! It really does remind you of our incredibly creative and powerful Creator God. We have truly lost something as Christians living in the city. I highly recommend it for all viewers, including those with children.

Once the movie started, Zeke did a terrific job. Julia held her ears and closed her eyes more than he did. There were actually several scenes which portrayed the circle of life. The funny thing was the way the different children interpreted these scenes.

One of the most intense scenes was a pride of lions chasing and ultimately overcoming an elephant. After the scene had ended (with a lion jumping on and taking down the elephant), I glanced at Julia, who looked like she had just eaten a rotten egg. She was horrified. My attention immediately shifted to Zeke. I was concerned to see how he would respond to the elephant's bad luck.

I was quite surprised as he looked at me, not with a sad expression, but with a big grin.

"They *got* it!" he said.

One Last Ride

41

It was May eighteenth, the day we buried my grandmother.
She was ninety-seven years old. It is strange to me how sad
I still feel, even knowing that our family had so much more time with her than
most have with their grandmothers. As we drove out of the funeral home parking lot, joining the other cars with FUNERAL tags hanging from their mirrors
and hazard lights blinking, I was intensely aware that this was her last ride.

As long as I knew her, Little Granny always loved riding in the car. She
was a member of that generation that understood simple pleasures. She would
happily accept an invitation to ride in the car just to "see what we can see." It
was only a few months earlier that we had shared a drive through the neighborhood looking at Christmas lights. Having lived in a small Tennessee town
most of her life, she was always amazed at the traffic in Houston where she
lived her last years. "Look at all the cars!" she would always say with amazement. I cannot imagine her ever getting a speeding ticket. There was beauty to
be seen along the road, after all. There were birds singing, blooming bushes,
trees budding with new leaves.

As our car continued down Columbia Avenue, we drove right by her
little stone house. A wave of sadness washed over me, and I was overcome
with tears. That house, in so many ways, represented my childhood. For a
brief moment, my memory went back to those days. Our road trips from
Alabama to that house would always end the same way: as we turned onto
Cleburne Street, I could always spy my granddaddy sitting on the porch,

eagerly anticipating our arrival. His eyes would light up when our car turned onto the gravel driveway.

"Mama!" he would shout as he stood up, "they're here!"

Within five seconds, Little Granny would appear out from the back porch, wiping her hands on her apron. There was always a delicious smell that followed her out the door—buttered oven toast or homemade chess pies or fried chicken. Little Granny's was a good place to be. And there was so much love in that little house, it spilled out onto anyone who entered.

Now as the funeral procession passed by, the stone porch sat vacant, except for the new tenants' stainless-steel grill. The back door did not swing open.

We continued our drive into the main square of Franklin, which looks much different now than when Franklin was Little Granny's home. There is a Starbucks there, where the Pigg & Peach used to be. A group of twenty-somethings drinking lattes paused in their conversation and looked up as we passed by. For a moment in time, new Franklin paid its respects to old Franklin.

On our last left turn into Mount Hope Cemetery, a construction worker took off his hat and held it closely to his chest. The man didn't know it, but Little Granny was indeed worthy of such respect, and so much more.

The children were silent in the back seat. Even as little children, they knew this moment was sacred. I fought hard against the urge to break the silence, and instead we shared in it, even as we shared our last moments together as four generations. My heart was full of mixed emotions as a mother. The desire to shield their little hearts from sadness was in conflict with the reality that these moments are a part of life that need to be experienced, even in the fullness and depth of sorrow that they bring. I knew that at that moment, I was modeling Christian grief for them. The silence was broken as I managed to say a little about heaven.

"We will see Little Granny again. Because of Jesus. . . ." These were the only words that would cooperate with my lips, which were tightly clenched for fear that a flood was about to erupt from them.

And then, our ride was over. Ninety-seven years was brought to a conclusion after our ten minute ride. Little Granny lived a beautiful life of faith. Even now, I still miss her. But I take great comfort in her faith and in my own. I imagine that somehow she participated in that ride along with us. And I also imagine that my sweet granddaddy is standing up on the great front porch of heaven right about now, joyfully anticipating his bride's arrival there.

42 Pottery Fun (Why Dads Get Ties for Father's Day)

I had a great idea for Father's Day this year. We went to a "paint your own pottery" place so the kids could make something personal for Michael and for their Papaw. Doesn't that sound like a terrific idea? Doesn't that sound like fun?

As we entered the overcrowded room filled with hopeful mothers and eager, messy children, we began the tedious process of choosing our pieces. This effort was quite frightful because of the tight fit between the wall of pottery and Zeke's burning desire to judge each piece by feeling it. To make matters scarier, each piece ranged in price from twelve to sixty dollars. Zeke has expensive taste. I was on pins and needles, but kept it hidden with my sweet mommy voice. "No touching, please, Sweetie."

One of the moms seated six inches from the wall of pottery caught my eye. Her little boy was painting everything black, bless his heart. We exchanged smiles of mutual admiration and understanding. We were both such good moms. This was going to be fun . . . and maybe a little challenging, too.

We selected our pieces and found a seat. I purposely chose a table that was completely empty, so that we could spread out. I know that my children break into fights when they are too close to each other; they are like gangs from the same city.

The lady who ran the shop came by to introduce us to our tools. She showed us the color wheel, with all the bright, cheerful colors that we could imagine. She showed us our brushes, each with a different level of thickness to fit its purpose. Last of all, she gave us a little sponge, called the "mistake sponge." She told us that we might not even need it. I think she and I both knew our little group would.

Just as we were getting started choosing our colors, the room began to fill up. We no longer had the luxury of our own space. Our family would be sharing a table with a very perky mom, who, I assumed by her tone of voice and unwrinkled face, was a kindergarten teacher or one of the Disney princesses. The children and I exchanged smiles of hello and returned to our task—choosing our colors of paint. This was where things began to go—well, let's just say—awry. For some reason, it seemed like a good idea to let Zeke have a say in the color choices. I always make the mistake of giving choices and then regretting it! Of course, Zeke chose black. The problem with black, as I would find out in moments, is that it covers everything else that you do. If you are a type B personality, this is not a problem. If you are a go-with-the-flow person, this is not a problem. If you came into this project with a blueprint sketch of what your children's artwork would look like—this is a problem.

I am not one hundred percent sure where things went wrong. Zeke went cuckoo. He was like a crazy three-year-old demon. In an instant, his hands were covered with black paint. He wanted to put his handprint on everything. I attempted to clean his hands. He got upset. He went limp to the floor and touched my leg on the way down. That was it for me. The devil took away the joy, joy, joy down in my heart . . . and left me with a black leg, a right-fully grouchy daughter whose careful artwork was now covered with a black handprint, and a now-screaming son on the floor. He had black on his face, black in his hair. He got off the floor only to soak our mistake sponge and cover our side of the table with blackish water. I wrestled it out of his hand and spanked him. There was not a mistake sponge in the world big enough to make this behavior better.

In the midst of this craziness, I glanced up to notice that the entire store was watching us. Meanwhile, the other family at our table was in another zone altogether. For every, "Stop touching the paint" and "You are ruining Daddy's present!" that came from my mouth, the kindergarten teacher mom would coo to her child, "What a great artist you are!" and "Wow, I love what you are doing there!" This only made me more self-conscious of the disaster that this had become for us.

We finished the pieces, although I cannot remember now how it happened. Divine intervention? The cashier told me my total, thirty-eight dollars. Julia mumbled that it was the worst day of her life. Zeke looked like it was the worst day of his life. I got tears in my eyes and mumbled something about how expensive the worst day of their lives was turning out to be. Another mom patted me on the shoulder and complimented the way I had handled things with Zeke. I think the paint fumes must have gotten to her, too.

Anyway, the worst part of all was that I couldn't tell Michael about it that night, because of the surprise factor. So now it is all out. Hope you enjoy your mug, babe! I *really* hope you do.

Manipulation
Tastes Like Jelly Beans

My daughter is ridiculously good at manipulation. Sometimes, she knows just what to say to push my buttons. Sometimes.

It all started when I told her if she asked for jelly beans one more time, I would not get her any. This was after she had asked me for about the tenth time in about half an hour. Seriously.

We made a deal. If she didn't ask again, I would purchase the candies for her. Can you guess what happened? Yep, she asked again. Unfortunately for her, she forgot that she had asked again. We got to the checkout line where the jelly beans are displayed and she began picking up each bag, reading off the flavor names. "Mom," she said excitedly, "these are all ice cream flavors!" I told her no and asked her to put the bag back on the shelf. I reminded her that she had broken her side of the bargain. And she was mad—mad at herself for breaking our deal—and mad at me for doing exactly what I said I would do.

And so began a litany of attempts to manipulate:

"I'm just stupid." (Our family doesn't say that word.)

"I'm ugly and fat." (Self-esteem card. Not going to work.)

"I look like something that a dog threw up." (My personal favorite. An attempt to make me laugh?)

"I will never eat anything else again." (I did answer this one with, "well, good luck on that!")

"I will just stay in my room forever." (hmmmm . . .)

"I hate jelly beans anyway." (Right.)

"By the way, I hate piano lessons." (Guess who her teacher is?)

For a moment, my mind left Julia standing sullenly with the jelly beans. I remembered another classic chapter from the manipulation textbook. Only this time, the star of the story was Zeke. He was potty training. Up until that point, if he ever called me in the night, it was for something important. Usually it meant illness or something that needed a mother's attention.

Up until that point, I had been able to trust him.

Then one night, I woke to Zeke yelling out fearfully,

"Mommy, I need you! I pell in the potty! Help!"

I kicked off the covers and sprinted to the bathroom where I found a frightened, wet-bottomed, shaking Zeke, stuck in the pee water of the toilet. I helped him out and cleaned him off. He was shivering. It was very sad indeed. I tried to calm him down and tuck him back in his bed. But, he was still shaking and cold. I just felt so sorry for him. So I broke our very sacred parenting rule, the one I have kept religiously since Julia was an infant, and I brought him into the bed with us.

I know, I know.

So, the next night I am awakened again with a similar cry,

"Mommy! I need you! I pell in the potty!"

I jumped out of the bed and once again sprinted into the bathroom. My poor baby. He obviously was having a problem getting the hang of this potty thing. What did my wondering eyes see as I rounded the corner to the bathroom? The picture on this night is not the same as the previous one. No, sir. You see, my angel had not fallen into the potty. He was sitting on the potty quite properly. He could have been a potty model. He looked up at me in such a suspicious way, I could almost see him raise his eyebrow slightly.

"I pall in the potty, I tuddle with Momma."

Yep. Just like that.

Only that night, I was not to be had. And now, standing in the checkout line with the most pitiful face looking at me, I could only think about winning this battle of wills. Julia tried one last attempt:

"This is the worst day of my life!" (Poor child. She has already had 147 this year.)

And with that, she was out of verbal bullets. This was followed by approximately three minutes of silence, almost as delicious as the jelly beans themselves. Then:

"Mommy, I am sorry for the way I have been acting."

I was impressed and slightly caught off guard by her self-awareness and her increased maturity. After all, I had not asked her to apologize. "She really gets it!" I thought, as I commended myself on staying the course. I had not wavered. I had not taken the bait. I had prevailed. The parenting victory was mine! I held back my urge to raise my arms and yell in triumph.

Proudly I responded, "Thank you, Julia. I accept your apology. I am proud that you decided to be a big girl."

She smiled. We shared a sweet moment of peaceful silence. Then:

"I think we should celebrate me being a big girl! I know," she said looking up at me slyly. "Let's celebrate with some jelly beans!"

44 "The Change"

In every woman's life, there comes a day when change happens. I am not speaking about menopause, although at this point in my life, I have nothing to lose there except perhaps the ability to maintain a steady body temperature. But I digress.

I am referring to the day when a woman must take a long, hard look in the mirror and realize she is no longer hip. Of course, the very use of this descriptor only proves that this is indeed the case.

I still remember my first dose of this reality. About two years ago I went into a CVS drug store to purchase something at ten times the regular price. (Old ladies are very frugal.) Behind the counter was a very good-looking young man. (Old ladies say things like, "young man.") Of course, I was sporting my new Forever 21 outfit, feeling very stylish and gorgeous. (You notice there are no stores called Forever 36—*way* too many numerals there.) Back to the good-looking young man. As he opened his mouth to speak to me, it was almost as if the words came out in slow motion. "A dollar, forty-two is your change, *ma'am*."

It still stings just seeing it in print.

Since then, I have had other moments of reality. I now use a daily facial moisturizer (because it really *does* diminish fine lines and wrinkles!) and thanks to two c-sections, I can no longer suck it in. Things that once stood proudly now have to fight bravely every day against gravity. I look ridiculous when I try to dance to anything faster than "Lady in Red." I actually contemplated getting a swimsuit this year with a skirt. I remember the song "Lady in Red."

Today was the final blow (besides death, which is probably the literal final blow). I got a speeding ticket.

It wasn't the actual process of getting pulled over that was new to me. I have been pulled over before for speeding. No. This was the first time I have *gotten a ticket* for speeding. Every other time I have been able to smile and "yes sir, Officer" my way into a warning—usually, a warning with a smile, or even a wink. Today, this thirty-six-year-old mother of two joined the ranks of all the other middle-aged women (or men of *all* ages, poor guys). I got the ticket. The officer didn't even crack a smile. Not at me anyway. He had the audacity to keep looking at the kids in the back, smiling and even waving to them, almost as if to say, "you guys may have an old mom, but you sure are cute."

I drove away from the scene and promptly set my cruise control on fifty-eight miles per hour. As I poked along in the slow lane, while *everyone* else in the city of Houston whipped by me, including several police cars, another epiphany! I flashed back to all the times I have griped about the old person driving super slowly on the highway. And I realized: they probably didn't even *want* to go that slow. They just know they, too, have lost their ability to negotiate and they are stuck in the depressing abyss of cruise control, too. I guess it happens to everyone at some point, right?

So, tonight, here I sit, sipping Diet Coke and watching recorded episodes of *The View.* As with most things these days, I find myself in the middle of the age demographic for this program—somewhere between Pampers and Depends. And, for now, I guess the middle is not such a bad place to be.

Now the big question: should I try my luck in traffic court or just sign up now for defensive driving?

45 One Man's Trash . . .

We had driven as far as we could the first day of our trip to Alabama. Five hours in the car had taken us as far as Lafayette, Louisiana. As the sun was setting, we began looking for a place to call home for the night. My budget mindset led me as I passed several recognizable hotel chains. We pulled into the driveway of the Cheapskate Inn, (this is not the real name, in case you look for it in the future) but I decided that since most of the clients there were standing around outside in the parking lot, we would just keep moving on. The Red Roof Inn seemed like a good idea. The sign outside boasted, "$49.99 and up," which was a language I could understand. Plus, the parking lot did not look like a scene from a drive-by shooting movie. This had to be a good thing.

On entering the lobby, we were greeted by a whole community of smiling faces on a wall mural. Underneath the smiling faces was a machine that would make coffee, tea, or hot chocolate. Julia and Zeke thought they were in heaven. They each got a complimentary Styrofoam cup and we toddled off to find our deluxe accommodations in room 205. First things first, Julia had to use the facilities. I was a little worried that the pillows on one of the beds looked a little bent in, kind of in the shape of a head, but I remembered all the smiling faces on the wall. Those new friends would say, "You're imagining things. Have some more hot chocolate!"

I went into the bathroom first to check it out. I was greeted this time *not* by smiling faces, but by a backed-up toilet with about ten cigarette butts swimming in it. To top it all off, like the cherry on this disgusting sundae of toilet, on the lid was the longest hair I have ever seen. I whipped around, and without explaining to the kids, we gathered our things and headed *back* to the happy lobby. Julia asked me what was wrong. I just explained with great excitement that we were going to "get an even better room!" The man behind the counter looked embarrassed when I explained the situation. I didn't blame him. It was not his hair.

He gave us the key for our next deluxe room, 209. This one was nice and clean. I was a little surprised to see the dark black carpet, but hey, I am sure there was nothing they were trying to cover up. The bed pillows were fluffy, which confirmed my suspicion that room 205 must have been rented by the hour at some point. No matter, the bathroom was clean and we began our nightly routines of brushing teeth, getting in pajamas, and tucking into bed.

It was after the lights went out that I saw the first one. In my peripheral vision, I caught something small running across the desk. I knew it was a roach, but it was just a small one. I managed to smack it with a magazine without drawing the kids' attention to it. Oops! There went another one beside the bathroom sink. Got him too. Another one on the wall beside my bed.

"Why did you betray me?" I asked the smiling people from the wall, although at this point I was suspecting mural fraud. The kids were asleep now. I tucked their covers under and around them, then around myself. "It will be like camping," I thought to myself, my optimism beginning to be replaced by something in the family of horror.

After about an hour of my eyes popping open to survey the walls around me, like a war veteran with Post-traumatic stress disorder, I fell asleep. Morning came and I suggested that we turn the lights on *before* we got out of the bed. The kids thought that would be fun, so we did just that. After enough time had gone by for little creatures to scurry off, we got out of bed. On the way out, Julia and Zeke had a second cup of complimentary hot chocolate from the magical machine. I glared at the smiling faces, which now looked more like mocking faces, to be honest. "Mom," Julia began while sipping her cocoa. "Thanks for letting us stay in such a nice place!"

On the way home, Mom and Dad slipped me some cash for improved accommodations. We stayed in the Quality Inn. It was beautiful and we slept great. Here are some things on my list to look for in a truly deluxe hotel:

Light-colored carpet ensures that your room was never a
       crime scene.
Shower curtains should actually be longer than the top
       of the tub.
Bath towels should be larger than hand towels.
Pest control is a must.

There was only one thing lacking in this second place. On our way out this morning, Julia asked, "Mom, can we get a cup of hot chocolate?" "They don't have that here, Julia." I answered.

As we headed to our free breakfast, I heard her mutter under her breath, "What a dump!"

The Note

Tomorrow is Julia's first day of second grade. Even as I type those words, I can hardly believe it is true. She is ready. She has new shoes and a brand new backpack with her name embroidered on it, thanks to Nana and Papaw. Her outfit for tomorrow (a navy knit dress with a cute apple pattern on it) is washed and hanging in the front of her closet. We have met the teacher, set out the new school supplies, and already identified an old friend who will be in the same homeroom. Julia has also placed her breakfast order for tomorrow morning—a special tradition in our family for the first day of school. The lunch box is filled and ready, complete with a note from Mommy, written on a small square of paper, which goes into every day's lunch all year. This is a tradition of which I am especially proud.

It began in kindergarten, with notes like, "I love you" and "I am proud of you." Last year, the repertoire was expanded to include short poems or behavioral reminders like, "Remember to listen more than you talk," and sometimes "*Please*, for goodness sake, make good choices today!" There is almost always a smiley face or a heart drawn on the note.

One day last year Julia asked me to stop putting notes in her lunch box. It nearly broke my heart as she explained that some kids in her class were teasing her about them. She said she was embarrassed. "Mom, I love you, but please stop." Though I was tempted to comply, I stood my ground. "I just can't do that, J. I want to keep writing you notes. It really means a lot to *me*," I insisted. Several days later, she told me that the kids in her class now thought it was cool, and that even if they teased her sometimes, she really liked getting the notes. Case closed.

As we stand on the edge of a new school year, I wonder what this year's notes will reflect. Life is getting more complicated for my little girl. In this new year, she will still need encouragement, but it will take on a new face. Notes like, "You're a superstar!" will make way for "Good luck on your math test!" Notes like, "Shine bright, sweet girl!" will make way for "Remember, be a good friend, even when it is hard." There will be days of celebration. There will be heartbreaks. Such is life. Even for a second grader.

Tomorrow's note? It reads: "A brand new year! What a gift. Start out on the right foot, and remember, you are loved so very, very much."

And, truly, she is.

Looking ahead a few years . . . will she still like my notes . . . even in junior high? Deep inside, I believe the answer is yes. Even if she protests. I anticipate that there will be days that she doesn't like me very much. Days when we struggle to speak the same language. Days when I "just don't understand." And I might not always understand. But I will continue to share my heart with her, one small, square of paper at a time.

Nobody does guilt like a mother.

I am not talking about a mother causing her children to feel guilty. Nor am I talking about constructive guilt, which leads us to a deeper level of self-awareness. I am not referring to the conviction that rushes over you when you respond to a construction worker's whistle with a smile, when you should have given back a look of shock and repulsion. (Sorry, Gloria Steinem, but I have been guilty of this in this past.)

I am talking about the completely unconstructive guilt that only a mother would subconsciously agree to take upon *herself*—the kind of guilt that causes her to relinquish control of her purse to her gum-starved four-year-old just to avoid a scene at the store—even when that child is naughtily chewing a piece for five seconds, spitting it out, and then getting a new piece. The kind which leads that mom to present a ten-minute sermon on good choices / bad choices at a higher volume than is necessary . . . not for the sake of the *child*, but for the sake of the adults who are giving dirty looks to the gum abuser . . . just so *they* will know that the mother *knows* the right thing to do. As if to say, "I *am* a good parent . . . just not right this minute."

The sad thing is, the more strangers look, the more desperate you get. The Mom-O-Meter inside your head is frantically ringing out the message: *you stink*! Even though, you know deep inside that there has been worse behavior within those same walls, many times before.

Recently, while waiting at Walmart's Vision Center, my children lost their minds. This was Columbus Day, and so, as I do on most school holidays, I had a preconceived agenda for the day. This agenda did *not* include my children losing their minds.

We entered the Vision Center as a respectable family. Sweet, even. We found an empty table and took our places in the chairs. A pleasant woman with a lazy eye (Seriously, working in the Vision Center. Wouldn't you think someone there could help her?) sat down to assist us. Poor woman. And I am not talking about the eye thing. She had no idea about the fun that was coming. I explained that we were there to get new lenses for Zeke's glasses. We handed over the prescription and got the process started.

Well, she had to call our vision insurance to verify the coverage. Apparently, that takes about fifteen minutes. This is not a long period of time when you are driving around in the car. But, in the Walmart Vision Center, it is an eternity. Like limbo, if limbo were filled with little frames delicately placed on fragile, little racks in an order that mattered greatly to someone.

So, the kids were great for the first five minutes. Then they found the display of glasses cases. There were pink ones, some with leopard prints, and some with cartoon characters on them, too. Right away, Julia started nagging me to get her a pink glasses case. I explained in my proper mommy voice that we were not there for a glasses case.

"We are just here to get Zeke's lenses," I explained. Cheerfully I added, "Maybe next time." Well, next time was not going to cut it.

"But Moooooooooom . . . I aaaaalways lose my glasses. This would heeeeeelp me."

Just for the record, in five years, Julia has never lost her glasses. I insisted that there would be none, and so she stomped off to the corner of the room to sit on the floor and pout and sulk and mumble comments about me. No biggie. I can ignore that.

Where was Zeke in all of this? Zeke was too busy realizing, with great delight, that the glasses cases could make a cool slamming noise if you push them together with force. Picture angry oysters. He also discovered that he could put his old tissues inside the glasses cases and then return them to the display case for the next customer to find.

Can you picture the scene? Norman Rockwell, eat your heart out.

I told Zeke to stop, which sent him into grouchy, temper-tantrum mode. He decided to walk through the Vision Center punching all of the mirrors on the walls and knocking tiny frames off their tiny stands. I quickly excused myself from the table, stepping away from Our Lady of Perpetual Waiting with the Wandering Eye, and scolded him up close. He talked back to me, "No, *you* stop." Oh yes, he said it.

At this point, the other couple in the store (too old to remember being parents, but not old enough to be grandparents) is staring at me like I have "Mommy-in-Training" printed on my forehead.

Never mind that there were children walking through the store with bare feet, eating McDonald's french fries in nothing but a diaper. At that moment, I was the worst mother in the world. I felt guilty. Feeling the weight of that guilt, that my children were disturbing the beautiful oasis of peace which was Walmart, I launched into a sermon. I had three points and everything. With a little more notice, I could have had a PowerPoint presentation. Desperate to achieve the illusion of control, which apparently ended once my children moved to solid food, I did it. I offered up my purse to the gods of chaos and moodiness.

The gum did the trick. But, oh the guilt. After all, I allowed myself to be bullied and I surrendered. I gave in! I knew better. I am still beating myself up, five days post-Columbus. Why do we do this to ourselves? Michael says that I judge myself so harshly because I judge others, too. I must admit, I have given mental parenting notes to many desperate moms I have seen over the past several years when I should have given a kind, understanding look instead. Or maybe offered their children gum. I guess the key here is to "do unto others as you would have them do unto you." In other words, don't dish out the dirty, judgmental looks if you don't want to get them.

Because one day, you might be the family staggering out of the Walmart Vision Center looking like you have been through a battle and with a disappointed second grader determined to lose her glasses at the very next opportunity . . . and a four-year-old boy, too busy chomping on twelve pieces of gum to talk back.

Happily, the rest of the holiday was great. And, as far as I know, the Vision Center is still standing. I only wish I could be a fly on the wall when some poor, unsuspecting customer opens their new glasses case to find . . .

48 My Girl

Time flies when you're having fun. That's what they say, right? Truth is, it flies no matter what. Even when you are not having fun. Time flies. This is an even more poignant truth when you have children.

My first born, Julia, is seven. (She would add "and a *half*.") At this exact moment, I am overhearing her directing Zeke in a play they are working on in her room. At this exact moment, she is being very patient with him and is enjoying his company. This could change, however, in an instant, much to Zeke's chagrin. Julia is crazy about her little brother. Julia is driven crazy by her little brother. This is how each day goes.

This year, she wants to be a veterinarian. She loves animals. On a recent field trip to the Outdoor Learning Center, her convictions were seen in full force. As the other children were handling and studying the pelts of different animals (squirrel, fox, sheep, skunk), Julia was having her own "sit-in" against the wall. While others were labeling, Julia was praying for all the animals who "lost their lives." Oh, the drama. That's Julia.

Sometimes, she blows my mind. She was always precocious and that has not changed. For a while, I thought she was going to be a tomboy. That part of her personality has definitely changed. She can often be found rummaging through my drawers, looking for jewelry she can borrow, or nail polish she can use. Since she is not allowed to have her ears pierced yet, she has started using glitter stickers on her ears. As she told me this week, "I really like fashion."

And she does. She puts clothes together that I would never put together. And, occasionally, it works!

I saw in her notebook the other day, "Samuel is so cute!" I am not eager for this stage to begin, and yet, I remember having mad crushes on boys when I was just a little older than she is now. Relationships with other children are getting more complicated these days. Some days on the way home from school, she will cry about a friend who "doesn't want to be friends anymore." One girlfriend recently told her she "wasn't pretty enough" to be in their cheer club. Girls can be so mean to each other. I suppose that truth will never change. Too bad. I wanted to scream, "You don't need their stupid cheer club!" But, I knew if I did, she would remind me that "we don't say 'stupid.'" So instead, I tried to change the subject to something different. She brought it back up. I gave my best advice: "You are beautiful inside and out. Be yourself. There are plenty of other girls to be friends with." Her reply said what she was feeling: "But, Mom, I really want to be in their cheer club." Oh good grief. I yearn sometimes for the early days when problems were solved with ice cream.

Time flies when you're having fun. And when you aren't.

I still check on her at night, before I go to bed. Her bed is usually surrounded with stacks of books. She can read anyone under the table. Funny thing is, I can barely remember her as a baby now. She is multifaceted now. Like a beautiful diamond. The bittersweet truth is—as much as I yearn to protect her from the world, from the mean girls, from the Samuels who will not return her affections, or the ones who will (Lord help us!)—those things will make her the woman she will ultimately become. She'd never believe me anyway, if I tried to warn her. She will have to live her life, make her own mistakes, learn her own lessons.

But, for now, she is seven. Seven and a half. She breaks my heart sometimes. She heals my heart sometimes. She's just like me. She's nothing like me. She's my Julia.

And oh, how I love my girl.

49 | Generation Gap

This morning I went to Bath and Body Works to pick up a gift for a friend. As I was paying for my merchandise, the perky, young cashier began telling me about their brand new fragrance. They have a brand new fragrance every time I come in. Eventually, they are going to run out of smells. They have already started mixing them into different combinations: mango melon, coconut lime, vanilla cherry. I suppose there is always room for combinations of three!

"Would you like a sample of our brand new fragrance?" the clerk asked cheerily. "It's called 'Country Chic'!" I have no idea what a country chic smells like, but I was honestly not that interested. I have a scent that I like and use, and I didn't really relish the thought of walking around the rest of the day with a country chic arm—just in case Country Chic turned out to smell more like country than chic. I am from the country, and let me just tell you, it doesn't always smell good.

"No, that's okay." I told her. I don't think she has been rejected very often, because her face looked more like Country Shock. Quickly, I tried to soften the blow. "I already have a scent that I really love," I explained. "I am already wearing it today and I just don't think anything could top it."

She looked pleased. At least I was a loyal customer.

"What scent is it?" she inquired.

"Sensual Amber," I answered, a little self-conscious that the name sounds like the stage name of an exotic dancer.

That was when she said it.

"Ohhhhhh. That one does smell good. That's one of our more, um, *mature* fragrances."

For those of you who may have missed the unspoken vocabulary lesson, mature means *old*.

Mature is definitely not Country Chic.

I am getting old. Not walker-old. Not adult diaper-old. But, middle-aged old. I remember another experience which proved this to be true, beyond a shadow of a doubt.

I went to see the *Twilight* movie. I went on opening weekend. I knew I was in trouble in the concession line. The giggling girl behind the counter asked the girls in line in front of me,

"Are you on Team Edward?"

"Yes!" they giggled back.

"Then you are going to *love* the movie," she said.

I was prepared to tell her that I was on Team Junior Mints, but she didn't ask me. She knew better. Or maybe she assumed I was seeing a movie for grown-ups. Not sure which.

The theater was filled with tweens and teens, all checking their phones for incoming texts before the movie started. "Surely they will stop doing that when the movie begins," I grumbled to myself as the annoying, glowing lights flashed to the left and the right of me. The only preview that appealed to me at all was for a movie starring Alec Baldwin and Meryl Streep. Another sign of my age. There were a couple of other previews, focused on some guy named Zac and another with the star of *Twilight*. These did not appeal to me at all, although the crowd around me seemed quite jazzed by them.

During the first scene of *Twilight*, Edward (the main character, who is a vampire) made his appearance. An ear-piercing squeal rose throughout the room. Girls around me were literally going crazy. Personally, I do not think that Edward is even cute. He's all pale and pasty. And kind of skinny. And slouchy. I was rooting for the competition. I lost.

The acting was horrible. Beyond horrible. The angst was so thick, you could barely cut through it with the annoying cell phone lights. There were half a dozen "almost" kisses during the course of the movie. Each time, we were treated to a loud squeal of frustration from the girls in the theater. Good grief.

The movie ended with a bit of a cliff-hanger. Personally, I am not hanging on the cliff. Because I *don't* care. As the ending credits rolled, the tweens and teens in the room clapped. They applauded. Ridiculous silliness. We filed out to a line full of fresh-faced kids waiting anxiously for the next showing. The girl behind me said perkily to the waiting mob, "You are going to love it!" I wanted to warn them, but I don't think they would believe me anyway. Kids hardly ever listen to old people. They would probably just roll their eyes.

So, I will not be attending the next *Twilight* movie. I have decided I can live without knowing what happens to Edward and Bella; although, if I had a mailing address, I would send Bella a big bottle of Country Chic. God bless them on their vampire life together.

As for me, I will just stay home curled up on the couch, smelling mature, and eating Junior Mints. After all, my life is probably half over.

And I'm okay with that.

Reading

50

Before the children were born, I loved reading. I enjoyed the classics. I also couldn't get enough of the Mitford series or *The No. 1 Ladies' Detective Agency* books. I read books on raising children throughout my pregnancies, so I could be prepared for the task of motherhood. Once the kids were born, I stopped reading. It wasn't a conscious decision really. My free time became time to catch up on my favorite television shows, none of which were rated-G, which made them unwatchable in the presence of the kids. My vision also changed after Zeke was born, making reading without glasses uncomfortable, laborious, and not very pleasant.

I am married to an avid reader. We both believe in the importance of reading, and so almost every Saturday we go to the public library as a family to get new books. Julia reads nearly thirty books each month. At the end of each visit, we carry our large stack of books to the checkout area: books for Michael, books for Julia, books for Zeke.

I should have known they were paying attention.

Last Mother's Day, I unwrapped Julia's gift, made in her classroom. It was a beautiful bookmark with her picture on it and a little poem about me.

"Sorry if you don't like it, Mom" she said, before I could even respond to the gift. "I *told* my teacher that you don't read."

Ouch.

I found myself in a new place this year. For the first time in my life, I don't have any physical New Year's resolutions. I have lost ninety pounds, I have braces on my teeth . . . outside of some plastic surgery, there is not much more to be done in that arena. So, I have looked deeper this year to some inner changes I desire to make. First on that list: read more books, watch less TV.

So, yesterday we took our Saturday trip to the public library. I didn't make a big deal out of it, but I picked out two books: one fiction, one nonfiction. We carried our large stack of books to the checkout area.

"What's that one?" Julia asked, as one of my books passed through the scanner.

"Oh, that one is for me," I replied, as casually as I could.

What came next, I will never forget, if I live to be one hundred. Julia and Zeke looked at each other and then at Michael, their faces filled with inexpressible joy. Then, Julia's joy erupted in one, loud sentence:

"Mom can read!"

Zeke was obviously impressed with my new-found literacy, because then they both broke the universal rule of libraries (the "shhh" rule) and began chanting loudly together:

"Mom can read! Mom can read! Mom can read!"

Laura Bush would have been so proud. So would my first grade teacher. I wasn't sure if I should take a bow or hide. I felt the urge to do both. Instead, I just asked them to cheer a little quieter.

It was quite a moment. By the way, I am halfway through my nonfiction book already. It is really good. Julia *told* me reading was fun.

Who knew?

Clinic Theology

51

There is nothing more sobering than visiting the Pediatric Specialties Clinic in the Texas Medical Center. Because Julia was diagnosed as an infant with congenital hypothyroidism, every six months we spend a morning in this place. The room is directly across the hall from the general pediatrics office. *That* room is relatively calm and quiet, with the exception of a baby's cry every now and then or the occasional immunization victim exiting the clinic. But our room, pediatric specialties is a different atmosphere. Today was no exception.

As we entered, my kids quickly gravitated to the TV corner, where Dora was already in the process of consulting her backpack for advice. My eyes scanned the room, partly from curiosity and also to see who we would be sharing the waiting room with for at least an hour.

There was a teen with Down syndrome, struggling with her mother, who kept repeating, "Stop that! Stop that!" In the corner was a set of grandparents, trying to pacify a young girl in a wheelchair by dangling Mardi Gras beads in front of her face as she tried to put them in her mouth. Every once in a while the girl would get mad, kicking her grandmother in the shins and screaming. I felt compelled to approach the grandmother and told her that she was doing a great job. She was so loving and gentle with her granddaughter, enduring her unintentional abuse with patience. She thanked me and seemed to appreciate the words of encouragement. She told me that her granddaughter is twelve years old. She has cerebral palsy *and* autism. Her mother died in a car accident when the little girl was one. So, the grandparents are raising her.

This would be grueling work for young parents. It is hard to imagine doing this kind of work well into your seventies.

During our conversation, two medical techs pushed in a little girl on a gurney. She had a feeding tube and a breathing tube. Her exhausted mother was following them, lagging behind, obviously longing for a break. I struck up a gentle conversation with her, in which she disclosed that her daughter was two. Her name is Madison. Because of her condition, she will likely never leave the bed. There were a couple of other kids in the room who had insulin pumps.

And then, there were my kids.

My daughter's hypothyroid condition puts us in the company of these others, even though, thankfully, her condition is fixed with a simple daily pill.

Environments like this cause me to reexamine my theology. It is hard to sit in a room like this and not feel blessed. I remember being in high school when I told someone that they were lucky. A well-meaning Christian adult corrected me. "No, not lucky . . . *blessed.*" I accepted that correction, believed it must be the holy way to talk, and moved on. I joined the Christian majority club, never talking in terms of luck, but rather, blessings. The problem that I face so many years later is, if you believe that you are blessed, then mustn't you be willing to accept that others are *not* blessed. In fact, many of these in the room today would surely be categorized as cursed. Can you have one without the other? Because I do not believe that God curses people, it seems more theologically sound to say "we are lucky" rather than "we are blessed." Would I, as a Christian, have the audacity to say to those other parents around me, "We are blessed?" Would that not cause the others to see God in a false light, as a callous puppeteer who shows favoritism? Is this the best way to profess faith to the world? Aren't our words more important than that?

The truth of the matter is, this is what free will looks like. We have to accept that God is either tinkering in our lives, or he is not. This, too, it seems, must be accepted fully or not at all. Can we expect him to act for us, and not for others? And then, what would be the implications of this belief as far as prayer is concerned? I do believe that one day he will make things right.

But this world is broken. This state of brokenness is why the specialty clinic was full this morning.

I will be the first to admit, I do not have all the answers. In Isaiah 55:9, God says, "My ways are higher than your ways" and I believe him! So, until I am further enlightened, I will give thanks to Almighty God for my healthy children. I will pray for those that I met today who struggle with their incredible challenges. And I will continue to grapple with my clinic theology.

52 Persistence

One of the attractions at Disney World's Hollywood Studios is "The American Idol Experience." Even before we set foot in Orlando for our family vacation, Michael had added the show to our itinerary. He knew the experience would be right up my alley. Tuesday was to be the day. After watching Julia go through Jedi Training Academy and fight Darth Vadar (after she engaged in a light-saber battle with him, she stuck her tongue out at him—spunky gal!), it was time. I must say, as I approached the entrance door with Julia (my moral support), I was feeling pretty confident. After all, I am not new to singing in front of people. I teach singers how to perform and I do have formal training and natural ability. So, with all the poise in the world, we entered the audition facility.

I chose to sing "Reflection," a Disney song that I had worked on with several of my teen vocal students. I knew the words and felt good about the range of the song. I watched a short video from Ryan Seacrest—ridiculously cheesy, but kind of fun, too—and then a hall monitor opened a door leading into a small audition room. Behind a desk sat a young woman who looked at me from across a laptop and asked me a few questions about myself. "Where are you from?" "What brings you here?" Then, she asked me to begin.

I sang for my allotted thirty seconds and glanced over at Julia, who was smiling proudly. I could hardly wait for her to hear her mommy being commended. Then came the verdict:

Rejected.

First, the woman told me that I did a good job, but she didn't think I was quite ready yet. She told me that I had some pitch problems. And then, to add insult to injury, she gave me a pep talk about how "singing a cappella is really hard." Good grief, lady. I am from the Church of Christ! For the first time, I could completely identify with the desperate audition candidates that we see on TV. I wanted to say all the things they say: "I can do it better." "Can I please sing something else?" "I *know* I can do this!" But I did not.

I handled all the constructive criticism with as much grace as I possibly could, knowing that my daughter was watching every reaction. The judge handed me my very own "I auditioned for American Idol" button with my name written on it . . . and we were shown the door. On the way out, all the nice hall monitors told me "good job trying!" and asked me if I had enjoyed my American Idol experience.

And I must say, I did not.

But, this was only Tuesday . . .

Time flew by and I didn't think about it again until Thursday morning. Right. Are you kidding? I obsessed about it almost every waking minute. What was that lady thinking? Couldn't she see that I have skills? I had to be better than most of the people who wander into her audition room.

This all may sound very conceited, but these were my honest, unspoken thoughts. I went back and forth between wanting to go back and try again and just letting it go. After all, who wants to be rejected twice? Plus, we were scheduled to go to the Animal Kingdom on Thursday and then take the shuttle bus to the airport at two forty-five that afternoon.

But, thankfully, the pull of Toy Story Mania was strong enough to help us change our plans. I also think Michael was slightly tired of hearing me bring up desire for revenge. I mean, for success. By slightly I mean somewhat more than slightly. By Michael, I mean my whole family. So, we boarded the bus for Hollywood Studios for our last day in Orlando.

After a fun time on Toy Story Mania, I casually told Michael, "I think I am going to try American Idol again. I will catch up with you guys in a little bit." He granted me the dignity of acting like it was just a whim on my part and gave me his blessing. "Oh, okay, babe. Good luck!" Then I set my course, and marched towards my destiny, prepared for the worst, but seriously hoping for the best, all the way softly humming up and down the scales.

As I approached the now-familiar entry to American Idol, the greeter went into the same speech as the first time. "Welcome to *your* American Idol Experience!" she said cheerfully. "Yes, I have had it before, and I did not care for it!" my inner child screamed. "Thank you," my outer middle-aged lady answered. I listened to her give me directions about what would follow, acting as if it were my first time. I know that is shameful, but I was feeling a little self-conscious that I had returned. I half-expected her to say, "Lady, you seriously need to let it go." So, I pretended. Sue me.

She guided me into the Ryan Seacrest waiting area, where I cringed upon hearing these words: "Hey, weren't you here a couple of days ago?" Ugh. The jig was up. Thank the Lord the first girl had already left, so I didn't have to explain my way out of acting like I didn't know what was going on. I decided to take the confident approach to answering that question. "Yes, I was," I answered with a big smile. "I decided to give it one more try!" Inside I was repeating, "I am *not* pathetic. I am *not* pathetic."

The poor boy looked confused, like he didn't know exactly how to handle me. "Um, would you like to watch the video again?" he asked. Apparently they don't have a lot of people come back for repeat visits. "No need," I said.

The judge was not back from a break, so I waited awkwardly with the confused hall monitor for a couple of minutes. I convinced myself that this was a great opportunity to model perseverance for my children (instead of just a chance for personal redemption) and held my head high as I waited.

The judge, Denice, returned from her break and brought me into the room, where I stood on the star (I know it is cheesy) and exchanged introductions. This time I decided to sing something from my own generation and sang "Alone" by Heart. I thought I totally nailed it . . . but I had thought "Reflection" was good, too. I braced myself and secretly crossed my fingers behind my back.

"That was really good!" she said. "A little more musical theater than pop, but good." I couldn't argue with that. After all, I am thirty-seven, and my "pop" fizzled out long ago. Some days, my pop feels more like plop, but I digress.

She asked me to sing another song from the list of pop ballads. Then, she asked me to sing another one. This was going well! Whoop! And then, the words I had waited for, dreamed about, *obsessed* over. "I would like to send you to the second round," she said.

Denice took me to the Coca-Cola waiting area, where I was to prepare using an iPod. This part was quite embarrassing because until that moment, I had never used an iPod before. After accidentally going to the main menu twice, I had to confess to the monitor. "Can you help me? I don't know how to scroll down." He looked at me like I was an alien. He didn't even know that I had come back a second time—that might have been worse. But, he helped me. I worked on my song a couple of times and then was introduced to the second judge, the producer of the show. The producer told me he liked what I did and then started another Ryan Seacrest video, in which he told me, "Congratulations! You are going to be in the show!"

The experience that was ahead of me was worth the wait (and the multiple moments of humiliation). First, I was told to return to the stage entrance an hour later. This would be time to work with a vocal coach, have my hair and makeup done, and run through the show on the stage. The other two contestants were very young: a seventeen-year-old boy, and an eighteen-year-old girl, both from the same high school. They still had their "pop." But I had a *heck* of a ballad.

Walking on the stage was such a surreal experience. The producer gave us our directions, we each ran through our songs, and then the audience started streaming in. Thankfully, I spotted my family, who had special reserved seating. The announcer introduced me. "And now, here's Melanie Simpson!" And out I walked. They showed a video clip of my "fans" which had been filmed in the lobby area. They were saying over and over, "Me-la-nie! Me-la-nie! Me-la-nie!" Seriously people, how many times in your life does something like *this* happen? The music started. And I sang!

I sang my heart out! The three minutes went way too quickly. And then, it was time to face the judges. There were three of them, just like on the show. A nice man, a nice lady, and a grumpy man. Their comments were pretty kind, although I was referred to as a "hottie Tupperware lady."

I chose to focus on the "hottie" part.

Then, the audience had a few moments to vote using a key pad. And the winner was . . . the seventeen-year-old boy. He had the most "pop." He also sang through his nose and really needed to get into his head voice, but he was full of pop. Sorry, I cannot turn off the critic within. I cheered for him, knowing that even if I *had* won, I wouldn't have been able to stay for the evening performance. After all, we only had one more hour at Disney and then we were heading to the airport. So, it was the best outcome for everyone.

As I left the auditorium to be reunited with my family, several of the audience members approached me. "You were really good," another thirty-something woman told me. Another one asked me if she could take my picture. All the attention was really kind of embarrassing.

Nope! It was *awesome*!

It was fun to see my family and talk to them about all the details of the day. The best part was being able to demonstrate to the kids the value of not giving up. Persistence pays!

And, I got a T-shirt to wear with my button.

The Baby Book 53

I love my baby book. As a child, I can remember two books that I never tired of looking through: my parents' wedding–photo album and my baby book. In light of this memory, I worked very diligently on my firstborn's baby book. Even the selection of the perfect book was a big deal. While Julia was still ripening in the womb, I had already begun the process of filling in the detailed pages. "Here's how we told our family you were coming" and "Your family tree" claimed many evenings as I devoted myself to this task. After the birth, I wrote in the names of every hospital visitor and every gift. I filled the book with the appropriate pictures, each with a caption elaborating on the memory. As Julia grew, I documented each milestone, and even kept a few pages updated with cute quotes. Julia was frequently surprising us with both her articulate speech and her quick wit. Julia's baby book is a masterpiece.

But, we have two children: Julia and Zeke. And Zeke's book is *not* a masterpiece.

Certainly, part of this can be attributed to the simple fact that Zeke is the second-born child. Zeke joined a family that was already in progress. He came into the world with a three-year-old sister and a busy and distracted mom. But that is not the primary reason that his book is lacking.

We began to notice Zeke's developmental delay at around five months. He didn't roll over and couldn't push up when he was on his tummy. I remember taking him in to the pediatrician at eight months and asking the new doctor there if I should be concerned.

"Zeke is not sitting up yet," I said with a nervous stomach. "When he does sit up, he topples over. Should I be worried?"

"Who's your regular doctor?" he asked.

I told him.

"Well, I am going to let him deal with this," he said very abruptly.

Then he handed me a brochure for ECI (Early Childhood Intervention) and thus began our bumpy journey into the unknown.

Every milestone was a triumph. But, none of them came easily. And, I suppose because of the fear and anxiety that I was experiencing, I didn't write anything down at all. I think in some ways, the bonding took longer with Zeke. Of course I loved him. But, I think I was keeping an emotional distance, at least subconsciously, to avoid being hurt. In hindsight, I should have been celebrating those milestones. At the time, I was just trying to check them off the list, like a child counting down days till Christmas or her birthday. Much from those months is a blur in my mind now.

Today, Zeke has grown into a wonderful, somewhat quirky, precious little boy. He has developed his own personality that is quite different from Julia's. He is playful and mischievous. He loves to play Connect Four and is pretty good at identifying where he needs to put his circle to block me from winning. He enjoys video games, wrestling, and "playing battle" with Daddy and he always sings a "da-da-da-da-da" song when he is happy. He is quite good at Lego Star Wars and can do a mean forward roll. He is learning to swim and still likes to cuddle with me at night while I read to him. And you know what? These things need to be written down.

So, during these summer months, when my favorite television shows are on hiatus, I am going to finish what I started nearly five years ago. The baby book.

And it will be a masterpiece.

The Mountain 54

Some mountains we can see. Some are in our minds. But climbing either kind is life changing. And exhilarating.

This week has been on our family's calendar since last month. This week, both of our children are enrolled in Crosspoint's Day Camp. Specifically, their Sports Camp. Zeke is going because he can always use more work on his motor skills. Julia is going because she has a love for all things sweet. Like me. Plus, Michael and I really want to encourage our kids not to fall into stereotypes. We want them both to be well-rounded. So, although there were other classes available, like art and drama, we chose to put Julia into sports.

Monday morning came! The kids had a great start. Both had an egg-white omelet with low-fat cheese and a banana for breakfast. They had a full glass of water. Sunscreen was applied. Healthy joy and potential filled the air!

Zeke was deposited at his pre-K classroom. No problem. As I entered the gym to drop Julia off, I immediately saw a potential problem. A room full only of boys. Correction—there was also one unfriendly (and unhappy) girl. To make matters worse, the boys appeared to all be in the upper range of the third- through fifth-grade age group. As Julia said, "Mom, these boys all look like Hercules." And so they did.

I kept a cheerful mood as I kissed her and bid her a good morning. Then I turned and walked to the door. I imagined myself in her shoes. Eight-year-old Melanie Fudge was terrified. And overwhelmed. And not prepared for this.

"You have a pretty face and a great personality . . ." I stopped the recording there. The one I remember. The one that crippled me as an older child and especially as a teen. Then, I reminded myself: this is a new generation. This is not Melanie Fudge. This is Julia Simpson. And her story will be different. I prayed a silent prayer for her. I had a lump in my throat.

I arrived back a few minutes early to pick them up so I could peek in on Julia. I scanned the gym as a lively basketball game was ending. No Julia. Maybe she was against the wall, out of my sight? Coach blew the whistle to call the kids in. No Julia.

The camp director called my name from behind the gym area.

"Julia is here," she said reassuringly.

I was, however, not comforted by this. She continued.

"She was crying after you left, so we moved her into art. There are *lots* of girls in there!" I began to feel the blood rising into my face. Julia came bounding out.

"Mom, I went to art and we made cupcakes! I had two! We made our own icing . . . blah, blah, sugar . . . blah, blah, yummy."

Honestly, at that point I had completely tuned out. I was seething. Not really at Julia. Well, not completely. At the lack of parents who signed their daughters up for sports. At my fear of continuing the "I can't do sports, exercise is bad, food is fun!" recording that played in my own head as a child and haunts me to this day. The one I fight every morning when the alarm goes off and I shake off the sleep to go out and walk. The one I fight every time I pass a Shipley's and consider stopping in. At the entire situation. What a debacle!

I asked about refunds. I asked about other options. There was a younger sports class, too. Maybe? We left and headed home, where the whole horrible story was retold to Julia's triathlete father, who also began to get red in the face right about the time that the two cupcakes were discussed.

Daddy did not offer other options.

"You are going to go back tomorrow, Julia. You are a strong girl and you can do it."

We compromised on the plan that I would ask about the younger class. Then Julia could have the choice. But, art was not a choice. We can do that at home . . . for *free*.

The next morning began as the day before had. Healthy breakfast. Positive attitudes. We marched in as climbers heading to Mt. Everest. Julia and I talked to both coaches. Julia did wind up having a choice between the two age groups.

"Mom," she said with fierce determination. "I want to stay with my age group."

I have never been more proud. So I thought. Turns out, picking her up at noon, I was more proud.

"Mommy! It was awesome! We ran a mile and played capture the flag!"

She also made a friend—not a girl, but a boy—and the coach confirmed that she had worked hard and had done a great job all morning.

This story will not make the news tonight. It will not even run across the bottom of the screen on one of the news channels. But this morning, in Katy, Texas, a mountain climber reached the summit. She is only eight years old. And although it won't make the newspaper, it will have a ripple effect for years to come.

And it was exhilarating. For us all.

55 Church in the Woods

I remember in college when one of my friends would miss church on a Sunday morning, the rest of us would tease about worshiping at the "Church of Christ at Fifth and Bedpost." It was just a joke, but the underlying sense was that missing church was something to be ashamed of—or at least was a mock-worthy offense!

I think I could probably count on both hands the number of Sundays I have missed church services. Today may have been number eleven.

We went camping this weekend. Since my job is no longer in professional ministry, I have the luxury of being able to be gone through a Sunday without any trouble. And our family had a wonderful time being together. Everyone was in a good mood. Even our dog, Zeus, got into the spirit, walking a two mile hiking trail on his four inch mini-dachshund legs! Michael and I sat in lawn chairs watching the kids chase fireflies as the sun set behind them. We ate s'mores and slept with the tent roof open under a sky full of twinkling stars. There was such a palpable sense of love and peace. The kids whispered to each other in the tent, "Goodnight, best buddy." Precious time.

This morning was Sunday. As a child, my parents made sure that we were at church on Sunday morning. Even on family vacations, I remember my dad sitting with the local phone book open in the motel room on Saturday night, looking for a place that we might join in worship the next morning. However, I also recall occasions when the phone book did not yield a beneficial option (I am being diplomatic, can you tell?) and we would instead have "family church." This usually consisted of my parents sharing a saltine cracker from the hotel restaurant and some juice and our family singing songs and having prayer together. Today was more like that.

As we walked down the trail this morning, we talked about this. Julia commented that one of her friends did not go to church and assumed that this meant she was not a Christian. I explained that while we do not know what her friend's family believes about Jesus, I was quite sure that going to church was not what *makes* you a Christian. However, church membership and attendance are *beneficial* for you as a Christian. I used the analogy of someone being healthy even if they don't exercise regularly. It is possible to be healthy without it, but it is an important ingredient in living a healthy lifestyle. If you are serious about your health, you most likely exercise.

I was glad to have this conversation now with Julia. There is such a fine line between diligence and self-righteousness. I had a flashback of myself as a fourth grader, informing my best friend and neighbor that I was pretty sure her family was going to hell because of their spotty church attendance. As you can imagine, this did not go over very well. I think I remember her dad coming over to talk to my parents. Obviously, I crossed that line.

This morning as we walked down the trail, our church service was a simple one. We sang a song about thankfulness. Everyone contributed a verse. We sang "This is the Day," which is one of our family's favorite songs. We held hands as we walked and admired the beauty around us. And that was it. It wasn't Fifth and Bedpost. It was Church in the Woods. And God was there.

56 Waiting Up

I remember the night vividly. As I tiptoed in the back door after my curfew, I was relieved to find all the lights already out in the house. It was not like I had been up to no good. I was just hanging out with some other kids from my church youth group. But, I was not home by midnight. The guilty panic that hit me as I walked toward the house did not discriminate based on the activities which preceded that moment in time. I had a weight in the bottom of my stomach the size of Michigan. I may as well have been out vandalizing nursing homes!

I turned the key in the lock as quietly as I could. No problem. However, as I began to pass through the living room, I spotted a lump on the couch. As my eyes adjusted to the light, I could see that the lump was my father. Gulp. But he was asleep. Relief. But, on his chest was a piece of paper which read, "Wake me up when you get home." Gulp. My first thought was to ignore the note and just go to bed. However, the longer I waited, the worse trouble I would be in. After all, I was only a few minutes late at this point. The longer I waited to wake him, the later he would assume I had gotten home. What to do? What to do?

Well, I woke him up. He told me he was glad I was home safely and that there would be a consequence to my missing curfew. It is funny—I don't remember anything else about that event. I have no memory of the consequence. But, I remember that note.

Years have passed. I am now the one at home waiting.

Julia had the unique opportunity to go the Renaissance Festival this weekend with a friend from school. The girl was having a birthday and wanted to celebrate by taking Julia and one other girl with her family to the Festival. Initially, we declined the invitation. After all, our family already had plans for the day. And, it was far away. And, we didn't know the family very well. And our default is usually no. But, after graciously declining, Michael and I discussed it. Julia has really been struggling with making friends. Rather, keeping friends. It seems that whenever she gets close to someone, they either move or we change churches. It has been hard. So, I called back and accepted the invitation. Julia was over the moon.

Saturday morning we drove her to the girl's house. Both Michael and I walked her to the door so that we could meet the parents face to face. Everything seemed kosher. We exchanged cell numbers and wished them a happy day. The car ride was very quiet after that. I won't speak for Michael, but I was nervous. Crazy nervous. What if this was just a scheme to abduct Julia? What if that girl was not actually their daughter at all? Crazy stuff like that. This was the first time that Julia would be gone a whole day. My controlling nature was short-circuiting. I considered tailing the group to Magnolia. However, we already had tickets to take Zeke to Dewberry Farm.

The girl's mom had told me that they would be back between four and five that afternoon. It was four-forty-five and Michael and I had heard nothing. I ran an errand, hoping that they would be back when I returned. Nope. Five o'clock came. No Julia. Michael asked me if I would call the number the parents had given me. I decided to give it another few minutes, not wanting to seem untrusting. I held out ten more minutes before calling. I tried to keep my voice calm and collected. The mom couldn't have been nicer. The day had been wonderful! And everyone was on the way, hung up a little by traffic leaving Magnolia.

I felt tremendous relief.

At six Julia came through the door, face painted with hearts and sunbeams, beaming from ear to ear. Her first big girl experience away from home was a success. Better yet, she really felt like she had invested a day in a promising friendship.

I thought about my daddy, sleeping on the couch with the note on his chest. I wondered what his thoughts had been as he drifted to sleep. Did he wake up occasionally to see if the note was still there? Was he as nervous as I was waiting?

I hugged Julia tightly and took in a giant breath. And then, finally, exhaled.

"O Come, All Ye Faithful"

Christmas is close. If you didn't know it already, it is evident as you skim the radio stations. Two of our Houston channels are already playing "all Christmas music, all the time." The kids have their favorites. Julia likes "I'll Be Home for Christmas." Zeke likes "The Little Drummer Boy." My favorite has changed from year to year. This year, my favorite is "O Come, All Ye Faithful.

It can easily be overlooked. It isn't as dramatic as "O Holy Night." It is not as peppy as "Jingle Bells." But the words spoke to me today.

"O come, all ye faithful, joyful and triumphant . . ."

There were several rough mornings this week with the kids. It seems that my always-cheerful, Prince Charming son has moved into a grumpy morning phase. Like Julia, his moods can turn on a dime. Most of the time, this is *because* of Julia. Three mornings this week, something she said or did set him off. Before I knew it, they were in a full-out verbal battle in the backseat on the way to school. Despite my attempts to speak softly and help them problem solve, nothing helped. I finished my pre-school-drop-off prayer ritual, even though Zeke was making noises through it as a sign of his disagreement with my loving words for Julia. This upset me and led to Julia jumping out at the school and running in the school doors, sad and distraught. I scolded Zeke and warned him to "turn it around," at which point he told me, "No, Mom, *you* turn it around." Well, I did turn it around—the car, that is. I parked on the side of the road and gave him three swats on the bottom. This sent him into the next phase of crying that went like this: "I . . . can't . . . stop . . . I . . .

can't . . . stop . . . I . . . can't . . . stop." Needless to say, by the time I had Zeke deposited at his school, I felt like I had been in a war. I was worn out. I had to fight back tears as I reflected on the morning. And then I was off to my full day of work.

"O come, all ye faithful, joyful and triumphant . . ."

On Monday, I am going to have an ultrasound. During my routine appointment with my ear, nose, and throat doctor yesterday, he noticed that my thyroid is enlarged. He suggested that I have the scan just to be safe. Funny thing is, that phrase never makes you feel safe. I have no need to be afraid at this point. And yet, as I scrolled through WebMD this morning, I began to feel exactly that.

"O come, all ye faithful, joyful and triumphant . . ."

Life can be so overwhelming. Relationships are precious and fulfilling—and exhausting. Our mortal bodies are fragile. Jesus' words from John 16:33 ring in my ears: "In this world, you will have trouble." Everybody over the age of one can say, "Amen. We get that!" But then he continues: "But take heart. I have overcome the world!"

There are days, many days, that I do not feel joyful or triumphant. Maybe you can relate. Maybe you even feel that way today, as you read this. I have dear friends who are facing this Christmas with broken hearts and broken bodies. But, it seems to me, in listening to the song with fresh ears, that these are not traits we have to muster up in our own strength. They are not prerequisites.

Maybe, just maybe, all we have to do is be faithful.

The joyful and triumphant will come from him, as we look past our situations. As we adore him.

The kids and I went for a ride in the car tonight to look at the lights in the neighborhood. As we drove and listened to Christmas music, my mind drifted to the concerns I have in my life. What will Monday's test reveal? What will Zeke's academic future bring? Will my business make it in this economy? How many more Christmases will I have with my parents? Oh, how I miss my Grandmother Locke during this time of year.

And then my song came on.

And as the radio began the familiar tune tonight, for a few minutes I allowed the words to sink into the broken places in my heart and in my faith.

"O come, let us adore him! O come, let us adore him! Christ, the Lord."

And with a faithful heart I sang along, joyful and triumphant once again.

58 Walking By Faith

We got a diagnosis on Zeke this week. After nearly six years of delays, therapies, questions, nagging suspicions, testing, and many, many prayers, we got a diagnosis.

Asperger's syndrome.

For those of you who may not be familiar with Asperger's, it falls on the autism spectrum. Children with A.S. have a few characteristic "tells": avoidance of eye contact, awkwardness in social situations, sensory issues, developmental delays, and inappropriate social behavior, like interrupting conversations or using an "outside voice" when an "inside voice" is clearly called for. The prognosis for children with this diagnosis varies, depending on the severity. Zeke's Asperger's does not seem to be that severe. But, one thing is for certain, he will have to deal with this his whole life. Asperger's does not go away.

So, I have done what any mother would do. I have been researching, reading, studying, making contacts with people who maybe can shed more light on what is to come. Yesterday, I was on information overload. I had a head full of knowledge and a heavy heart. So, I decided to do what I usually do when I am feeling overwhelmed. No, not eat a pie. Very funny! That was the old me. I laced up my tennis shoes and went outside for a long walk alone.

It was an especially windy morning, as a front was coming through, bringing with it some much-appreciated cooler Houston weather. As I started out down my street, I felt almost as if I were pushing against a wall. I had one in my heart, too. As I walked and pushed, I processed and prayed.

"Why does this have to be his road, God? He is such a sweet little boy. Why?"

What will this diagnosis mean for Zeke? Will he be able to have meaningful relationships with friends? Will girls like him or break his heart? Will he be able to marry one day? Will he be bullied? Will his life be sad? Adolescence is hard enough on its own. How would this be exacerbated now?

I feel so helpless against this and ill-equipped for what lies ahead. How can I possibly be the best mom for Zeke?

I picked up my pace and started to jog into the wind. I felt almost angry that my relaxing walk was becoming a chore. But the wind was not going to win. I was not going to back down. I found a rhythm in my breathing. I jogged harder.

That is when it dawned on me. That is precisely why I am the right mommy for Zeke.

I am a fighter. I am tenacious. And so is Zeke.

When the kids were very little, Michael decided to paint each of us a picture one Christmas. At the bottom of each special painting, he chose words to write, as an almost prophetic blessing for each of us. Mine is about my beauty (smile). Julia's is about her ability to bring light into the darkness. Zeke's is about being a fighter.

> *"Zeke, the lion.*
> *He conquers all challenges placed before him,*
> *and all those around him are blessed by his roar."*

Truly.

I smiled as I thought of that painting and relaxed back into a walk. The Bible talks about walking a lot. In it we read commands to "walk in obedience," "walk humbly," "walk in the light," "walk in love," and my favorite, "walk by faith." Interestingly, "walk by faith" is found in 2 Corinthians 5, in a section about the struggles that we face while in our earthly bodies, and the great, immeasurable joy that will come when our mortal bodies are replaced by the glorious immortal.

"We walk by faith and not by sight."

What we *see* is overwhelming. What we *see* brings fear. Love casts out fear. Faith breathes hope into our hearts.

Faith that no matter what the future brings, Zeke's beautiful eternity has already been secured by Jesus. Faith that nothing, no, *nothing*, can ever rob him of his relationship with his Lord. Faith that the earthly love of his family will sustain him. Faith that his name is carved on the palm of God's loving hand. Faith that God has not made a mistake. Faith that He will be with us every step of the way. Faith that Zeke will bless others with his testimony, perhaps *because* of this. Faith that one day, Zeke will look Jesus right in the eye and tell him how much he loves him.

After thirty minutes of struggle, I finally reached the turnaround point. I could feel the difference immediately as I rounded the corner to begin the two mile trek back to my house. I was moving my feet, but it was as if the wind were carrying me home.

So, on I walked. "Being therefore always of good courage . . . for we walk by faith, not by sight" (2 Corinthians 5:6a-7 ASV).

How to Heal a Broken Heart

Remember the joke that starts like this? A man walks into the doctor's office and says (while banging himself on the head), "Doctor, it hurts when I do this!"

Julia wants a boyfriend. She is eight years old. While these two sentences together are horrifying, right now it is also very innocent. I don't think she would know what to do if she had one. She's just enamored of the concept.

On Wednesday, as she was recapping her day for me, she confessed that she had written a note to a boy in her class. We will call this boy "G." In this note she explained that she had a crush on him and asked him if he felt the same about her. There was a yes box and a no box (remember all this???). Well, the boy was an overachiever and made his own box: absolutely not. Julia was crushed. And embarrassed. After my initial reaction of "You did what?" followed by an explanation that she was too young to be giving boys notes of this nature, I sat down on the bed with her. This was, after all, a great opportunity to bond with my budding tween.

I can surely relate to her heartbreak. So, I stepped down from my elevated mommy box and actually set out to communicate with her, woman to soon-to-be-woman. When I was in sixth grade, (note—*not* third!) I had a crush on a boy in my math class. He sat in front of me. I would daydream about couple skating with him and kissing him . . . all while staring a hole into the back of his head. As I am typing this, I think I just realized why I am not good at math. I thought he liked me a little bit, too, because he sent me a carnation on Valentine's Day when the student council sold them as a fundraiser. Turns out, he just wanted to support the school's purchase of a new sign outside, because the carnation meant nothing to him. He had sent *twelve* carnations to a new girl who was also a cheerleader. She was beautiful. And, she could skate backwards like a teenager, not just holding hands side by side (the dorky way to couple skate). I was insecure and heartbroken. I really thought he liked me. Did the dollar he spent mean nothing? I digress.

I told Julia that I cried many a tear over this boy. And, while it was not appropriate for her to write notes to boys, I always wanted her to feel comfortable coming to me with what is on her heart. And, that to the best of my ability, I would listen and share my own stories with her (note—when they would be beneficial. I have a few too many stories.) I prayed for her aloud and we read 1 Corinthians 13 together and talked about what love should look like when it does happen.

In short, we had a moment.

"Mommy, I really feel sad because I really liked him," she said through tears.

"I know, J. It will be better tomorrow."

Apparently, it was.

So, last night (that would be Thursday if you are keeping track), she casually mentions to me that she was really sad about what another boy wrote her on a note. "What boy are you talking about?" I asked reluctantly. "G?"

"No, Mom. Not G . . . N. I *really* like N."

"What are you talking about? Did you write *another* note?"

"Yes, I told him that I have a crush on him."

"You did *what*? We just talked about this *last night*! Remember that Daddy and I both said not to do that again?"

"Oh, I forgot. Oh no, do you have to tell Daddy?"

"Yes, I do. I cannot believe you did it again. What did N say when he read your note?"

Wait for it . . .

"He said I need to cool it with the notes."

I waited a moment so I would not laugh. "Well, Julia, I couldn't have said it better myself."

There was no moment of bonding this time. Just a consequence. I did tell her that I will always love her, though. Even when she does really dumb things. That's what moms are for.

So, here's hoping she will stop writing checks hoping one will get cashed. And I hope this boy-craziness will not get too much worse in the years to come. One thing I do know for sure—there will be many more heartbreaks.

But you certainly don't have to go looking for them.

So the doctor says to the man, "Then stop doing that."

Exactly.

60 Magic

I do not have magical powers.

But, every once in a while, I can actually see my words coming out of my mouth in slow motion. It's amazing, really.

Zeke has been having a lot of tantrums lately. (Michael says he has not seen any. Pshaw!) I suppose Zeke has been saving "the drama for his mama." Yesterday, he got set off in the morning when I had the audacity to tell him that a ham and cheese omelet and toast with peanut butter was enough food for his five-year-old stomach. "I am still hungry!" he argued. Within three minutes he was sobbing in the car, kicking his feet. "You are so mean, Mom. How could you tell me that I am not hungry? You don't know. You (sniff) don't (sniff) know (sniff) *anything*!" I did show him that I knew how to drive *and* reach behind me and swat him at the same time. It was quite a charming moment, as you can imagine. He had some other issue in the afternoon, although I must have blocked it out of my memory, because for the life of me I cannot remember what it was.

Last night we had special friends over for dinner. We had not seen them in several years and I really wanted to make the most of the visit time. After saying the prayer with the kids, we sent them to their rooms for bed. Typically at night, I read Zeke a story. Last night, I just thought we could skip it. I should have known better than to tamper with our routine. As I broke the news to him that there would be no story, he started up "You are so mean, Mom (part 3)." There were tears and everything. "You (sniff) always (sniff) read (sniff) me (sniff) a (sniff) story!" he began. He was starting to get louder. I did not want our friends to hear this. The sound of his usually sweet and precious but now incredibly whiney voice literally made my brain ache.

(Pause the parenting DVR for a moment.)

I know the right thing to do in this situation. You never negotiate with terrorists! You cannot let them win. You cannot let them smell insecurity. I know the right thing to do.

(Resume)

My eyes began to scan the room for the shortest book I could find. *Goodnight Moon* should do the trick.

And then . . . the magic happened. I leaned over his face and whispered in my most authoritative (and yet still pleading) voice. And I could actually see the words coming out of my mouth in slow motion.

> "If
> you
> will
> be
> quiet
> I
> will
> read
> you
> one
> story!"

The devilish smile that crept across Zeke's face told me all I needed to know. We would get through this quickly, but I had lost the battle.

Rats.

Now if I could only figure out the magic in getting him to forget that this moment ever happened.

61 The Birds and the Bees

Julia turned nine this year. Here is the state of the union: as frightening as it is to me, she is already interested in boys. She confessed to a friend's son at a New Year's Eve party, "I have a crush on you." Thankfully, it was not reciprocated this time. The poor boy went running with fear. But one day soon, it might be mutual. In addition, the statistics tell us that girls are entering puberty much earlier than they did when I was a girl. Judging by the pediatric PMS that I have witnessed over the past year, I believe that we may be thrust in the middle of pubescent fun within the next couple of years. And Julia needs to know what she is up against. So, after much deliberation, Michael and I decided that this was the right year to talk to her about the facts of life.

I do not remember my parents ever sitting down to teach me about sex. Part of me is glad, because I would have been absolutely mortified. This would have most likely been a mutual mortification, which is probably why it did not happen. I do remember going to a special presentation in fifth grade, where the facts were presented to us. The boys were separated from the girls and we were shown a filmstrip about the basics: menstruation, breast development, how to use a maxi pad, and more. It was horrible and somehow empowering at the same time. After the film, the nurse asked if we had any questions. We had a million, but of course we only responded in giggles. On our way out the door, we were given a goodie bag containing a trial-size deodorant stick, three gigantic pads that could have absorbed the Mississippi River, and a couple of the tiniest tampons you have ever seen (for the very brave).

Filing out of the classroom, we could not look the boys in the eye. They teased us that they knew what we had been taught. I don't believe it for a second. After all, we didn't know anything about what they were taught. We did notice that the boys' goodie bags were much smaller than ours (lucky boys). But the hallway smelled like Old Spice for a week after the presentation. I learned about most of the facts that day from the nurse, and of course, with the supplemental help of Judy Blume. I never did talk to my parents about sex—even when I really should have.

I want to have open communication with Julia as she grows up. Whether it makes me uncomfortable or not, I want her to always feel free to come to me with questions and concerns about her body. So, I set out to find the perfect book to start the conversation. Off I went to the budget bookstore.

"Do you have books for teaching your children about sex?" I asked the clerk.

"Oh boy. Time for that, huh?" she joked. "Follow me. We have a whole section."

And they did. I skimmed through a couple. The first one was written for teaching much younger children. Too immature. The second one presented not only the facts about traditional sex, but also options. Way, way too many options. Some of them would have made Bill Clinton blush. I would never use this book! I felt like Goldilocks after the first two bowls of porridge. Then I found *just right*. It was full of the important information, but did not open unnecessary cans of worms.

Feeling quite proud of my purchase, I took my book home. After dinner, I invited Julia into her room and began reading the book with her. Having the book really helped. I still found myself biting my lip at times so I would not giggle, but being able to stare at the book when I felt the giggles coming on really helped me stay on task.

My plan was to stay on a very narrow road. I would present the most pertinent information and that would be that. As the Jedi fighter instructed Luke Skywalker, "Stay on target." Problem was, Julia kept asking questions that took us to the next level. I should have known she would. Smart kid.

The book said, "the husband and wife fit together in a very special way . . . and the sperm and the egg are united." Julia wanted to know, "but exactly *how* did the sperm get to the egg?" So now I had to talk about ejaculation. Worse, I had to say the word "ejaculation."

The book said, "this is how a husband and a wife make a baby." Julia wanted to know what to do if you and your husband don't *want* to have a baby. So now I had to talk about birth control.

The book said, "husband and wife." Julia wanted to know what would happen if you and your boyfriend wanted to "fit together in a special way." Oh brother.

She wanted to know about childbirth. She wanted to know if she could get pregnant and not know it. She wanted to know about tampons . . . and how to use them . . . and if she could see where the babies come out. I declined that request, by the way.

I wanted to scream, "May-day! May-day!" and run to Mexico. But I didn't.

I just let her ask what she wanted to ask. And I answered honestly, with as little detail as possible. I was sweating a little. She was having the time of her life. Once we were done talking about it all (nearly an hour later), she wasn't nearly done.

"Mommy, can we talk about this some more tomorrow?" she asked.

"Absolutely, J," I answered, "but there is not much left, sweetie."

I don't know if it was a burning quest for biological knowledge *or* just having something secret to keep from Zeke, but for several nights after that, she would call me into her room.

"Mom, I need to ask you something . . . you know, about our girl stuff."

And I would go in. And we would end up rehashing something from another night.

So, now she knows all about the birds and the bees. And looking back on it now, I am proud of the way it went. I don't think I could have done any better. And she was most certainly an attentive audience. Now I will just continue to pray for her, that she will be a godly and respectable young woman. I pray that she will be comfortable in her own skin. I pray that she will hold sacred this special gift from God. And I pray that she will come to me, when she needs to talk about these matters.

And as I pray, I am thankful. Thankful for the relationship that we are building with each other. And thankful that when it is Zeke's turn, it will be Michael holding the book.

62 Confidence

It was my kindergarten program. I was going to sing a duet with my best friend, Ashley. "Doe a Deer" was the selection. I remember rehearsing it many times. The big day arrived and I emerged from the curtain in my frilly dress and took my place at the front of the stage beside Ashley. I looked out at the audience. And then . . . stage fright.

"You start it," I whispered as I nudged my friend with my elbow.

"No, you start it," she rebutted with a slightly more powerful elbow nudge.

It became clear after about three more rounds of this verbal tennis match that neither of us was willing to pave the way for the other. Around the time that the audience began to move from amused to impatient, I got the giggles. Don't get me wrong. I had the skills. But I lacked one thing. Confidence.

It appears that my daughter is not missing this gene.

The kids have started gymnastics. Zeke is built like a gymnast. Julia needs the coordination that gymnastics will provide. One thing she does not lack is confidence.

The girls' team was working on the balance beam this week. There were six girls. Quickly you could see that five of them knew what they were doing. It was not their first week! They had such poise and displayed skill in walking the beam, toes pointed with each step. Then there was Julia. It was her first week after all, bless her heart. She was wobbling back and forth with every forward step. Then, just when she was getting the hang of it, the instructor asked the girls to walk the beam *backwards*! Double bless Julia's heart! Her teacher saw the potential danger of Julia's long limbs swinging back and forth and moved her to her own beam. My heart felt heavy as I imagined the embarrassment she might be feeling as she made her way to gymnastics Siberia.

On the way into the facility, Julia had commented to me, "Oh Mom, I came to a birthday party here. This is going to be so *easy*!"

Flash forward to my sweet little teeter-totter, arms flailing as she tried desperately not to fall off the beam, again. I worried a little about how she would feel about the experience as the class concluded and we all walked to the car.

"Great job trying your best, guys! I could really see you making progress!"

Zeke answered quickly, "Mom, that was *hard*. But I love it! I want to be in the Olympics!"

Julia was quiet for a moment. I thought about trying to give her a little more of a pep talk. Turns out, it was not needed.

"Mom," she began. "I think my teacher could really see my potential."

"Oh really, J?" I inquired. "Why do you say that?"

"Well," she began, very matter-of-factly, "the other girls had to all be on one balance beam. She gave me my *own* balance beam. She could see how good I was."

And I may be overly confident in my parenting, but I think I was a very good mother at that moment.

I kept a totally straight face.

63 War and Peace

The kids have been bickering a lot these days. The battles seem to come out of nowhere. One minute they are singing "we're best friends forever." The next minute they are plotting ways to get revenge. Julia has actually memorized the scripture verse: "'Vengeance is mine, I will repay,' says the Lord" (Romans 12:19 NASV).

She quotes it to Zeke quite a lot. I think she is missing the point of the verse, but hey, the kid is memorizing Scripture.

I have tried many things to break up their bickering matches. I have sent them to their individual rooms. I have taken away things they enjoy. I have tried to broker peace using a gentle and calming tone of voice. This always worked for my dad. For me, not so much. I think when I use that voice the kids think I might be an alien, as this is not my personality type. I have yelled and threatened. This sometimes does work, as it results in my looking ridiculous and the kids' bonding through their mockery of my "mad face." "Mommy has her mad face. Mommy has her mad face."

The latest battle began at a restaurant. I had decided to treat the kids to lunch. Very soon it became apparent that it would not be a treat. Zeke wanted to pick our table, and had chosen a two-seater. This would have been a perfect selection if he had been on a date. However, there were three of us. Julia also wanted to pick our table, and had chosen a lovely corner booth with enough room for us all. Did I mention that Zeke does not like to lose? I tried to prevent strife by choosing a third table option, just so no one would win. Alas, it was still seen as defeat. Zeke blamed Julia for our not sitting at his table. Julia blamed Zeke for my having to choose a third table. And so it began. Quickly, it escalated from "I wanted to pick the table!" to "Julia, you are so stupid. You are the meanest sister on the planet!" Julia shot back with "Get away from me, Zeke. I wish I were an only child!" Then we could use the two-seater, but I did not interject that fact (didn't seem helpful).

Soon, they were in an all-out war. Harsh words were flying like darts. I was irritated, because I really just wanted to enjoy my salad in peace. What to do? What to do? Since I imagine myself to be a fine Christian parent, I was not surprised that a wonderful scripture verse came to mind. This time it was not "Vengeance is mine . . .", but instead, "Love your enemies and pray for those who persecute you" (Matthew 5:44 NASV).

"Guys," I began, "we are going to try something new. I want each of you to pray and thank God for one thing about each other."

Immediately, my mind imagined what might follow. "Thank you, God, for my stupid sister." "God, please help my dumb brother stop being so stubborn."

So, quickly I added, "and it cannot be sarcastic. You must thank God sincerely for something about each other."

They both stared at me blankly. But they agreed. And so we began our prayer. Julia: "God, thank you for Zeke. He really is my best friend."

Zeke: "God, thank you for Julia. She is a great sister."

Me: *"Amen!"*

No sooner had I articulated the "n" sound, they were hugging each other. It was a miracle! We ate our food with smiles and no one got indigestion. It was beautiful. I had found the solution. This vacation to Utopia lasted through a bowl of soup, a salad, and a fruit cup. They were walking out holding hands, the lion and the lamb, in perfect harmony.

Julia reached into her purse and popped a gumball into her mouth.

Zeke: "I didn't get a gumball!"

Julia: "Sorry, Zeke, I don't have another one."

Zeke: "Julia, you are so mean!"

Me: "Dear God, here we go again."

64 Married to an Ironman

My husband is an Ironman.

I have always been amazed by him, since the night we met. He impressed me right away with his kindness and the manner of respect that he showed me. Okay, well, *first* with his broad shoulders, muscular legs, and blue eyes; but *really*, the kindness and respect were right after those. I met him after a long relationship that had ended in heartbreak and betrayal. It had been almost a year since that relationship ended. I was not looking for another guy. But, I met Michael anyway. He blew me away after only a few minutes together. I could tell immediately that he was the real deal. He was easy to talk to. He was a gentleman. I actually asked him what was wrong with him on the night we met. I assumed there must have been a flaw for him to be single. There was not.

I told my roommate that night that I thought I had met "the one." Now that I am older, I will tell you, I don't believe there is a "one." Although this does not sound very romantic, I believe there is a large number of men that I could have committed to and lived a relatively happy life. However, I am so proud that I chose wisely. For once in my life! In fact, the morning after the Ironman, I bragged to my mom and dad, "I married a winner!" Truth is, this was just as true on our wedding day as it was after the race.

Michael did not have the beautiful childhood that I was blessed to have. He has never used that as an excuse to be less than what God created him to be. God planted within him at a young age a drive to succeed and a desire to hold himself to a higher standard. God planted within him a seed of self-discipline, mental fortitude, and commitment the likes of which I have rarely seen in another human. He does not look for the easy way out. He does not shirk challenges. In fact, he seeks them out. He puts his nose to the grindstone for as long as it takes. And then, he conquers the challenge. And he comes out stronger than before. This is the way he lives his life. He does what he says he will do. He is faithful to complete everything he begins. He willingly makes sacrifices for the good of our family. In a world full of big, spoiled, little boys, Michael is a man. This is why he amazes me.

After months of hard work with training and diet, the day of Ironman Texas arrived. He methodically checked each hurdle off his "to do" list. First, a 2.4-mile swim. Next, a 112-mile bike ride. Finally, a marathon (26.2-mile run).

The kids came to the race with my parents in time for the marathon. They had made posters that read, "Go Daddy!" and "Michael Simpson . . . Ironman!" They had little tambourines and lungs ready to yell. And that is exactly what we did. And then we would wait for him to finish the eight mile lap when we would see him again. We had lots of time to wait in between the laps. For me, this was a time for observation and for reflection. We watched a man run by on a prosthetic leg. We saw a blind athlete who later finished the race, the entire time tethered to her assistant or perhaps a very, very devoted friend. And during this time I thought about my own little family. Our obstacles are not easily visible. But every family has them—things that weigh them down. As a mother, I worry about what my children will face in life, Zeke with his Asperger's diagnosis; Julia with her highly sensitive and emotional nature. But on this day, I worried about Michael. What in the world would I do if he didn't make the deadline? What would I say, as his wife, that could possibly give him any comfort? I worried. But as I reflected on this, I could hear Jesus' words, even over the noise of the cheering triathlon fans:"Therefore I tell you, do not worry about your life. . . . Can any one of you by worrying add a single hour to your life?" (Matthew 6:25, 27).

I know this is true. But as we waited for what seemed like an eternity for Michael to come back around on his last lap, I confess, I had a heart full of worry. And if that worry *could* have added an hour to my life, or at least to the finisher clock, I would have gladly donated it! Would he make it in time?

The finish line was like something from a movie. He had told me, and many others, that he would achieve his life dream of crossing the finish line, or he would go off on a stretcher. I deeply hoped it would not come to that. With eager eyes, we watched the big screen that projected the path leading to the finish line. And, then . . . looking like a warrior after nearly seventeen hours of struggle, there he was.

And as our children screamed, "Daddy, you did it! Daddy, you did it!" I knew in my heart we had all witnessed something profound and sacred. A moment that I will never forget. A moment that will stick with our children as they grow and struggle and face their own challenges in life. We were all able to see from the outside what goes on inside the heart of a champion. There was pain. There was sacrifice. The odds were against Michael. He just kept putting one foot in front of the other. He pressed on, step by step. He would not accept defeat. He never surrendered. He succeeded. And a part of us succeeded with him.

When he crossed the line, only five minutes before the midnight deadline, the announcer, Mike Riley, proclaimed to everyone who could hear it those magic words, "Michael, you are an Ironman!"

But I already knew that.

No Good Deed . . .

65

You have probably heard the saying before. I have always disliked hearing it actually, because, as an optimist, I don't want to agree with it. No good deed goes unpunished. I would much rather promote the concept of pay it forward or something cheerful like that. But sometimes, like it or not, the sentence is true.

About seven months ago, right around dark, we had a knock at the front door. Generally, my husband answers these late night knocks—opening the door a crack and scolding gruffly, "There is no soliciting in this neighborhood." On this particular night, he was already relaxing in his boxer shorts, so I did the honors. One thing you should know about me, I am a softie. I always end up listening to the whole sell job before I tell them no. Or, when I am feeling even softer, I tell them I need to talk to my husband, take their card, and leave them with a grain of hope, and a big smile. When I was in high school, a guy came to the door of our house signing up people for home water delivery. He was extremely cute . . . and who doesn't need water? So, of course I signed my parents up for a contracted year of service. (You're welcome, Mom and Dad.) The lady at the door on this evening did not know my history. But, lucky for her, she got me.

"I am from Kid Help," she began cheerfully.* "We are an organization that helps children living in poverty in the United States and around the world. Would you like to look at some pictures of our children?"

Oh boy. This would be even tougher to turn away than water.

Almost immediately, I made a connection to my own childhood. One year my family had sponsored a child through a similar organization. Our little boy was from India. His name was Serm. My brother and I, both around middle-school age at the time, found the name humorous and quite unfortunate in its similarity to the word "sperm." Snapping back from my reminiscence, I realized quickly that I was smirking a little. Fueled by my desire to make things right in honor of Sperm, um, Serm, I asked the lady to tell me more about her organization.

I caught a glimpse of one child's face on her clipboard. And that was it. I signed all the paperwork, authorized a draft from our account each month, and then called the kids to the door to help me choose our "adopted" child.

We found a little boy in Mississippi named Bryson. Zeke liked that he was around the same age. Julia liked that he was photogenic. As a deeply patriotic veteran, Michael would like that we were assisting a fellow American citizen. So, that was that.

I halfway expected him to mock me for being a sucker, but Michael didn't. I explained that I would use my allowance each month to cover Bryson and that the kids would do chores around the house to help contribute towards the cause. Bryson took his place on our refrigerator and I found a place in the kids' nighttime prayer to insert his name.

For five months, we prayed for Bryson. Then, on a Friday, I received a packet in the mail from Kid Help.

"Thank you so much for sponsoring Prince," the note read.

Prince? Who in the heck was that?

I went to the website and sent an e-mail. "What happened to Bryson?" I asked. "My kids have been praying for him for five months," I explained.

"Bryson is no longer in the program," they answered. "We hope you will consider sponsoring Prince."

It had to have been providential, since his first name was my favorite musical artist from the 80s and his middle name was my brother's. So, I agreed that we would sponsor Prince and asked that they send us his picture to put on the refrigerator and some information about him so that the kids could feel connected. In the meantime, there were some problems with the automatic draft. The organization lost some of the paperwork, then they charged us twice (which they refunded later). We got loads of correspondence from them, sometimes duplicates, sometimes conflicting messages.

"I don't think they know what they are doing," I told Michael, as I put Prince's slightly less photogenic face over Bryson's face on the fridge.

The kids had a much stronger response that night as the prayer was amended.

"What happened to Bryson?" they questioned tearfully. "Did he... die?"

"Oh goodness, no. He did not die. We just have a new boy now, so we will put his name in the prayer."

"But we don't *want* a new boy," they whimpered.

I didn't blame them one bit. How could Kid Help do this to us? I knew it was not their fault that my children were going through this turmoil, but I still felt frustrated that their sense of choice had been taken away. I took the opportunity to make it a teaching moment and we talked about how all helping is good.

"God knows the situation that each child is living in. He is in control. Perhaps this new little boy needs our help more."

They listened politely, but did not look convinced at the end of my elegant and faith-filled soliloquy. That changed a few days later when we got a letter in the mail from Prince.

"Thank you for choosing me! I love trains and puzzles . . ." The letter was short but precious. And we all bonded with our new boy, albeit through the mail.

The bubble popped, however, with the arrival of a new letter from Kid Help.

"We are sorry to hear that you have decided to stop your sponsorship. However, you can rest assured knowing that we have already found another family to sponsor Prince . . . blah, blah, blah."

So, after seven months, two amendments to the kids' prayer, and two refrigerator photos, we are no longer partnering with Kid Help. Looking at the situation as a mother, I am frustrated that my children may have learned "no good deed goes unpunished." My prayer is that years down the road, they will only remember the two boys whose names were included in their nighttime prayers, wedged between the names of family members and close friends. Perhaps that memory of gracious acceptance will be the takeaway. I am sure that at least for a while, their names will continue to be lifted up in my children's prayers. Something tells me that Prince might find a train or a puzzle under his Christmas tree this year.

I am not giving up on charity. I will continue to look for good deeds to do. I believe that no good deed is ever wasted. Still, for the time being I will just ask Michael to answer the door instead.

*The name of the organization has been changed.

A Poopy Situation

66

It was Zeke's turn to get new glasses. We had planned the outing for Friday after school, since it would take several days to get the insurance worked out and the prescription faxed from his eye doctor. As Zeke is usually pretty decisive and low-maintenance in terms of appearance, I assumed that we would be able to get in and out quickly. Besides, there are not as many choices for boy frames as there are for girls. After trying on five pairs, Zeke settled on a pair of blue frames, with a little bit of green on the inside. They were quite handsome and I was happy to purchase them, although they were a little over our budget. It was about this time I noticed that Zeke was giving me the universal, male sign of "I need to go to the bathroom."

"Zeke, stop doing that," I instructed quietly. "I think you need to go potty."

"I could try," he agreed. For Zeke, who almost always rejects the suggestion to go to the restroom, "I could try" translates to "I am about to explode if I don't go pee in the next minute."

The nice lady helping us with the order seemed to sense the level of need and offered up the staff bathroom for Zeke's relief. Thankful to have an older child to help out, I asked Julia to please escort her brother to the back room and to wait for him to finish his business.

Minutes went by. Out came Zeke, still giving me the universal sign.

"Did you go??" I was baffled. "Where is Julia?"

"She had to go, so I still haven't gone." He looked pained.

"Tell her to hurry up so that you can have a turn," I instructed.

He disappeared for another couple of minutes and then came running out. I knew by his face (and his hand still on his crotch) that the issue had not been resolved. I thought he was going to tell me that he had had an accident. The news, however, was far worse than that.

"Julia said to tell you . . . the potty is overflowing."

Oh Lord.

The nice lady at the desk (who appeared to be about eighteen) smiled awkwardly as I excused myself to investigate the situation.

What I saw. . . oh, the horror.

The evidence stood out like a sore thumb in the all-white, staff bathroom. Sure enough, the brown water had risen to the rim of the bowl. There was one brave, little trickle of brown water coming down the side and across the floor to the drain. Julia looked very embarrassed.

"I tried to use the plunger, but it didn't work." My sweet, responsible daughter had tried to remedy the situation. Bless her heart.

"Don't worry, sweetie. Plungers can be tricky. Mommy will be able to get it."

I scanned the room for the plunger. It was then that my eye fell upon the cleaning brush, sitting beside the potty in a bowl of brown water. The bristles were brown. It must have made a lousy plunger.

I desperately looked through all the cabinets. No plunger. My mind began to race. And even though it was an accident and not my poop, I began to feel embarrassed. I would have to explain the situation to the manager.

This was not the first poopy situation I have found myself in with Julia. Although the last one was many years ago, I still remember the occasion vividly. She was a baby. If you have raised a baby, you will remember that every so often, they have what Michael and I refer to as a "blow-out." These are the poops that seem to never end. Julia decided to have one at a party. The hostess, a gracious and lovely woman, had a house full of expensive furniture. Most of it imported from Russia. Seriously. I tried to be discreet as I gathered up the diaper bag. Julia needed a change. Quickly.

"Where is the best place to change her diaper?" I asked the hostess politely.

"Oh, you can just do it on the couch!" she said casually.

So I set up shop on her all-white, Russian couch.

As I fastened the Velcro on the diaper and began picking up the changing mat, I heard a sound in Julia's fresh diaper that reminded me of avalanche movies on TV. But this was not snow coming down the mountain. Julia was having a blow-out.

I waited until the avalanche ended and got out another diaper. As I put it under her, it became clear that she was still not finished. I grabbed for more wipes. I would wipe. More would come. I would wipe. More would come. I put another diaper down. And then another. I was horrified. I wondered how many frequent flyer miles it would take to get to Russia. How do you say, "I need a new, white couch" in Russian? I was sure I would have to find out. Four diapers later, it was finished.

By some miracle, the couch was not harmed. But I still felt embarrassed.

So here we were again, nine years later, in another poopy situation. And Zeke still had not been able to go potty.

I wondered how many people actually saw me enter with the kids. I also quickly wondered if a rooster would crow if I denied knowing them. Too bad for me. It was not very crowded. And my children look just like me.

"I am so sorry," I began. "My daughter has stopped up your toilet. You guys don't seem to have a plunger, so I am going to run to the store and get you one. In the meantime, *please* don't let anyone go in there."

Zeke was getting crabby. Kids tend to get that way when their bladders are about to explode. Julia was self-conscious and moody. I was feeling angry. Half of me wanted to drive away and never come back. But, we are getting limited in our vision center options these days. (Remember Walmart?) We couldn't burn this bridge too, even if the bridge *was* over a nasty, brown lake of poo! I also knew that this was an opportunity to demonstrate taking responsibility for our actions. So, I ignored my inner child who was screaming, "I am so embarrassed I will die! Go! Go! Go!" We all piled in the car and raced over to the store.

Julia took Zeke to the restroom while I speed-walked my way to the bathroom supplies. I grabbed up a four-dollar plunger and a four-dollar cleaning brush / bowl combination and raced back to the cashier. Julia and Zeke were just coming out of the restroom.

"Let's go, guys!" I cheered. I was beginning to get my second wind. The adult in me was winning.

The three of us all piled out of the car and charged into Eye Masters like the SWAT team. I glanced proudly at the manager as I raised the bag of "goodies" into the air slightly. I wanted to whistle the Mighty Mouse theme song, but I did not.

The bathroom had an "Out of Order" sign taped on the door. I was relieved to know that no one had stumbled upon the gruesome scene while we were gone. I found a pair of disposable gloves in the bathroom cabinet and set about my work. Within five minutes I had successfully cleared the toilet, cleaned the floor and thrown away the dirty brush and bowl. As I set out the new equipment, I felt a twinge of pride at the way that I had handled the situation. Somehow, I was able to keep my daughter's dignity intact throughout the experience. I must have said fifteen times, "You didn't do anything wrong. It was an accident."

In the end, we all walked out with our heads held high. I had a sense of satisfaction as a mother. Zeke had a sense of relief. And Julia? Well, she felt a couple of pounds lighter. And in the car, there was a unified peace of mind. After all, we have at least one more year until someone else needs glasses.

Breaking the Law

67

I should have known the situation was serious when Julia came running into the room. She was holding the phone out in front of her body like it was a stick of dynamite.

"Mom, Zeke called someone!" she said frantically. "They are still on the phone!"

Although I am not a rocket scientist, I knew the solution to that problem. Assuming he had dialed a random phone number, I took the phone out of her hand and casually pressed the "end" button to conclude the phone call. About that time, Zeke came prancing through the living room, grinning from ear to ear. Mischief was definitely afoot.

"What did you do?" I asked him.

"Nothing, Mommy," he answered in a singsong voice. Out of curiosity, I pressed the redial button.

911.

I could feel the blood draining from my face. What would this mean? Julia never did this. New territory.

"Zeke, you called 911? That is *very* serious! Why did you do that?"

"I wanted to see if it would work."

A sound reason. But, obviously, this was not acceptable. It was, however, about the time that Julia took a one-way trip to crazy town.

"Oh no! They told us in school that when you do that, your parents get arrested! Mom, are you going to get *arrested*?"

I assured her that I would not get arrested. I sincerely hoped I would not get arrested. I also hoped we were not about to be bombarded by a slew of emergency vehicles. We have never experienced this before, and I wasn't exactly sure what was going to happen. But I knew I could never make it in prison. I am *way* too high-maintenance. I thought I was convincing in my reassurance. Julia wasn't buying it.

"What do we do?" she screamed. It was like a scene from a movie, when the Mafia has a dead body in the house and they know the cops are on the way.

"I guess you can start praying that the police do not come," I answered, albeit sarcastically. And that is exactly what she did. She ran into her room and threw herself prostrate across the bed crying and praying aloud. Incredibly loud. It was reminiscent of her hospital performance during Zeke's stitches.

"Oh God! Please help us!" she pleaded again and again. It was quite dramatic. Like something out of *Steel Magnolias*, but without the comic relief.

"Julia. You have got to calm down. You are acting like we are in a *real* emergency. Everything is fine. Nothing is going to happen."

It was about that time that we heard the knock at the front door.

The police officer was very friendly as I opened the door. "Is everything all right here, ma'am?" he asked politely. "We always come after the second 911 hang-up." That stinker had done it twice! Or, was the second call the result of my redial? Hmmm. Didn't matter. I was certainly not taking the blame on this one!

I explained the situation to him—five-year-old boy, blah, blah, blah. He seemed very understanding. I am sure it was not his first experience with fake 911 calls. I wanted him to see that everything was okay, so I invited him inside. I did not realize that the usually beautiful "Welcome" decoration that I have hanging from the front entry was askew. In the movies, this would make the police officer suspicious that there had been foul play. I glanced at the officer casually as we passed the wall decoration. He did not look suspicious.

"Would you please talk to him?" I asked. Thinking this would be a great way to drive home the point with Zeke, I ushered the officer into Zeke's room. I wanted the man to see the Biblical posters on Zeke's wall displaying the Ten Commandments and the Armor of God. "See. We are good people! We are law-abiding citizens!" I wanted to scream. But I did not. I thought I would just let Zeke's penitence speak for itself. Yes, Zeke's penitence would speak volumes about his upbringing.

What we saw there was both shocking and embarrassing. It was most certainly not penitence. Zeke did not even look sorry. He looked happy and proud. I suppose he was relieved to find that 911 actually did work. Maybe he was proud that his action had brought about an exciting response. I don't know what the child was thinking. But he was dancing and singing. He was not intimidated by the officer. Meanwhile, Julia was crouched in the corner rocking herself in the fetal position and hiding her face.

This did not look like a suspicious situation at all. No, sir.

I tried to get Zeke to stand up straight and look the officer in the eye. He wasn't having it. He squirmed out of my grip and fell limply on the floor, giggling all the way down. The officer told him that it was not a good choice to call 911 unless there is a real emergency. Zeke mumbled "sorry" to him and I walked the officer back out to the front porch.

"And this is only the first day of summer vacation," I lamented to the officer.

"Looks like you've got your hands full," he said sympathetically. "Good luck!"

Great. A police officer who deals with juvenile delinquents is wishing me luck with my children. I shifted uncomfortably, then reached up and adjusted my "Welcome" decoration. Proud moment.

My parents never had such a moment. My brush with crime came the summer before my fourth grade year. And it was a secret moment between me and God. My dad had sent me on an errand to the grocery store next to his office building to buy him a Diet Coke. He had given me enough money for the soda, but nothing more. Standing in the line, my eyes were drawn to a pack of orange Trident gum. At that moment, I stopped thinking clearly. I remember taking the pack of gum and putting it into my pocket. As I paid for the Diet Coke, I felt flushed. Reminiscent of Edgar Allan Poe, I knew the cashier could hear my heart beating out of my chest. She did not. I made it out of the store, hands sweaty, heart pounding. I kept walking. As I approached the edge of the parking lot, my conscience kicked in. And, as this was clearly a crime I was committing, my conscience was speaking in the King James Version.

"Thou shalt not steal."

I thought I could ignore it.

"*Thou shalt not steal.*"

I could not.

I turned around and walked back into the store. I put the gum back on the shelf, unopened. And that was that.

Unfortunately, "thou shalt not call 911 for fun" did not make it on the top ten list. If it had, I am quite certain that Zeke would have done the right thing. After all, he has the Ten Commandments hanging on his bedroom wall. Did I already mention that?

I suppose as long as he is never the subject of a 911 call, or the cause of one, I will just be thankful. And, maybe I will sleep a little more securely tonight, knowing that 911 really does, in fact, work.

Redefining Me

68

On March 16, 2007, I had finally had enough.

We had taken church directory photos in January. What I saw shocked me. I didn't know who that woman was in the picture. It was certainly not the way I saw myself. Physically, I was in the worst shape of my life. I was tired all the time. My feet hurt, just from normal activity. That morning I was horrified to realize that I couldn't reach around myself to wash my backside in the shower. Emotionally, I was in the worst shape of my life. I felt defeated. The hill seemed too steep to even attempt to climb. I remember telling Michael, "This is just who I am. I am just meant to be fat." I weighed in at almost 240 pounds. I marked the date on a journal that I kept hidden in my bathroom cabinet. March 16, 2007. The day I finally had enough.

I had dieted throughout my entire life—beginning in fifth grade. That was the year that Chris Beiman began teasing me about my weight. He called me "Fudge Melon"—a creative insult taken by combining my name and my shape. It was a stupid name, but it hurt my feelings something awful. He called me that all the time. As a result, I was probably one of the youngest consumers to purchase Slim Fast, back when it was a disgusting powder. I had great success in college with diet supplements (later discovered to be very dangerous) and rigorous exercise. This regimen gave me great wedding photos, but was short-lived, as most quick-fixes are. Again, in our first years of marriage, I had great success. This time I worked with the Weigh-Down Workshop, a Christian-based support group curriculum. But, once I came to a different place theologically, the magic was gone. I could not believe that my overeating was causing Jesus pain; although, pain was a result. Pain and shame. They were mine.

Time went by. Four pregnancies. Two miscarriages and two live births. Each bringing with them pounds, either from depression at losing the baby, or from comfort food that helped with the nausea. Both babies arrived with different concerns, both of which started me on a path of emotional eating. During my c-section with Zeke, the doctor, at our request, shut down the "baby shop" once and for all. For the first time in five years, my body was completely and totally . . . mine. This contributed to my decision that day. I had no more excuses.

It's embarrassing to try to justify to other people, "I just have a little post-pregnancy weight."

"How old is your baby?"

"Um . . . five."

Why share all of this with you? Because I want you to know, reader: I understand. I want you to know. It *is* hard. I want you to know. You *can* do it.

It took me two and a half years to reach my goal. Now I am happy with the woman I see in the mirror. She looks like me.

But something was still missing.

Growing up, I would have never considered myself an athlete. Just seeing that in print makes me giggle, remembering the struggle that I had completing the Presidential Fitness Tests in school. Do you remember those? The worst part was the BMI test. The PE teacher measured the body mass index with a set of pinchers. The girls would line up in the locker room and watch as the teacher would find the most tender places on your arm and waist and then pinch them to reveal your percentage of body fat. It was as horrible as it sounds. Painful inside and out. It always revealed that I was deficient. By several inches.

In sixth grade, I tried out for the volleyball team. I was excited at the news that I had made the call-backs! But, serving the ball overhand was not one of my strong suits. I did not make the team. My name was scratched off the list. And in my mind, "athletic" was scratched off of mine.

I gravitated to choir after that, where I found my niche. It would be years before I ever ventured into the world of tennis shoes again.

Last year, I watched my husband cross the finish line at the Texas Ironman competition. He defied all odds, as he looks more like a linebacker than a triathlete. But, he put in the work. And he did it! I have been telling him for years that he "inspires me." One morning as I was walking around the neighborhood, it hit me. "You inspire me" is only the beginning of a sentence. Inspiration has to look like something. It has to result in something. I had to find the ending to that sentence. And I wasn't going to do it watching TV.

It was sign-up time for the Houston marathon and half marathon. Michael suggested it one morning.

"I think you should sign up for the half marathon," he said with a totally straight face.

"Are you kidding me?" I answered suspiciously. "I hate running!"

"Well, you used to hate running. But that is all a decision. You have a different body now than you had before. I know you can do it."

I was extraordinarily skeptical, but agreed to think about it. The lottery would fill up. A decision would need to be made quickly.

It was with fear and trepidation that I checked my e-mail on the day that the lottery results were announced.

"Congratulations!" the e-mail began. "You have been chosen to participate in the Houston half marathon!" I had found the ending to my sentence and was honestly surprised by it. It would be: "You inspire me to run a half marathon." Gulp. I had imagined it might be a five kilometer. This competition would require much more of me. But I was willing to take the next step. The kids were excited for me. When I say "for me," I not only mean "on my behalf" but "in place of me," as well. I was terrified.

Michael suggested that I join a running club that he had joined several years ago when he ran his first marathon. So, I signed up and bought my first pair of running shorts. The night before the first run, Julia put a small note in my hydration belt pocket. It read, "Go Mom! Keep going! You can do it!" I posted that note on my mirror. I still look at it every day.

I showed up on the first day with a stomach full of nerves. I made several rookie mistakes right away. I showed up a little too late for the parking situation and missed the main group take-off. I found a woman to run with, but took off way too fast, trying to stick with her at a pace that really pushed me out of my comfort zone. But, I did it! It was a two-mile run.

I have been running for about two months now. Even in that short time period, I have seen myself growing stronger and faster. Best of all, my children are watching me take this journey. My daughter is proud of me. And perhaps she will be inspired by my actions and example. Because, as it turns out, I am a runner! Who knew? Certainly not me. Although the half marathon is not until January, I am certain now that I will accomplish it. I am sure it will be a profound experience as I cross the finish line, with my source of inspiration by my side. It seems almost poetic that the race will take place the weekend of my thirty-ninth birthday, nearly three decades after I decided that I was not an athlete.

This past week, I ran nearly five and a half miles without too much trouble. As I was walking back to the car, I was overcome with emotion. I almost could not tell the difference between the sweat on my face and the tears falling from my eyes. They were tears of pure joy. I had finally exorcized the painful memory of Fudge Melon. I had buried her with my volleyball disappointment and with those terrible pinchers. I was redefining myself. "Take *that*, Chris Beiman," I thought as I drove home.

Michael, Julia, and Zeke were waiting for me when I got there. "Yay!!!" they cheered as I walked through the door. I stepped into the door, into the applause, and into my new identity.

The Problem with Brothers

69

No one can get to you like a brother.

Don't get me wrong. They can be really fun when they are little. I had so much fun dressing my brother up like a girl and directing (bossing) him in countless plays and impromptu performances. I actually have a tape recording of us playing radio disc jockey as little children. Of course, I had all of the speaking parts, but Jeremy got to push the record button. At one point on the tape his sweet, high-pitched voice can be heard contributing a song title. This is immediately followed by my louder, firstborn voice complaining,

"Momma, Jeremy is ruining our tape!"

I am not sure how highly *he* would rate those memories on the fun scale, but they were certainly fun for me. Brothers are also handy scapegoats when you need one. But at some point, they grow up, and develop the ability to say no and to stand up for themselves. At that point, they become a problem.

I have a picture from my ninth birthday that tells the story. I was having a party with the board game Clue as the theme and all my friends had come dressed as their favorite character. My brother was only seven, but even at that young age, he gravitated to my friend Shannon who was dressed as Ms. White. Let me refresh your memory. She was the French maid. The picture shows all of my friends standing in a line waiting to be judged for best costume. My brother is grinning from ear to ear, practically stuck to Shannon's feather duster. And on the end of the line is me, Ms. Scarlett, staring a dagger into his head. It is a hilarious picture. Now. For some ridiculous reason, probably just to include him, my mom had appointed my brother to be the judge of the costume contest. Well, guess who he picked? Even at age seven, he knew a hottie when he saw one. It was totally not fair. My poor friend dressed as Colonel Mustard never stood a chance.

In middle school, I remember having my brother tag along with me on lots of outings: to the movies, to the pool, to the skating rink. The only saving grace was that my friends and I could make fun of his striped knee socks. And we did that a lot.

But things got much more complicated once his voice changed.

One day, out of the clear, blue sky, one of my girlfriends called on the phone. Assuming she wanted to gossip about her latest crush, I was on my way to my bedroom with the phone. I was stopped in my tracks when she said these words,

"Um, can I please speak to Jeremy?" I made her repeat herself.

"Jeremy?" I questioned.

She confirmed her request. It was a very awkward moment for everyone. Except Jeremy. He was pretty jazzed about it as I recall. My friend would later end up going on a date with my brother.

Was I in a nightmare? Nope. Brothers!

Time went by. My senior year of high school, I was stuck taking PE my last semester. Can you say, "procrastination?" By some twist of fate, my brother ended up in the same class with me, along with the other eager freshmen who were actually excited about physical fitness. One of the requirements for the class was a one-mile run at the end of the semester. This was not my strong suit. Jeremy finished quickly, along with the rest of the class. I felt increasingly self-conscious as the track emptied out, leaving only me, huffing and puffing around the track. If I had been him, I would have felt humiliated. After all, everyone there knew we were related. There were not a lot of Fudges in our high school. And I was not exactly the picture of health and vitality. He would have even been justified in laughing at me—payback for the knee socks, you know.

Instead, he started running beside me.

"You can do it!" he cheered as all of his friends watched. "Keep going, you are almost there!"

I finished the mile run, thanks to his encouragement. I cannot remember if I even thanked him for that. But I never, ever forgot it.

And there were other moments like that one; moments when my biggest fan was my brother. Even when I had a car accident while driving him to his first big dance. His date was upset about her dyed shoes, as we had to spend some time standing outside while waiting for the tow truck to arrive. My brother was concerned about me. His date decided it would be better for her to hitch a ride with some other friends to the dance. My brother stayed with me as I talked to the police officer who arrived at the scene.

He was always quite the critic where my boyfriends were concerned, too. I don't think he really liked any of them, until Michael came along. He was right about that one.

Recently, I had a health scare. After a needle biopsy of my thyroid, I had to wait an excruciating week before finding out the results. I thought it might be cancer and I was really scared. My brother called me on the phone to share a word of encouragement and a scripture verse with me. We talked candidly for about an hour about the issues we were both dealing with at that time. There was instant comfort in talking with Jeremy, because after all, we are family. He is my brother. And that relationship is precious.

This is one of those many lessons that you cannot teach your children. They will just have to discover it for themselves. Thankfully, Julia and Zeke already enjoy each other's company, most of the time. They have weekend sleepovers in Julia's room. They call each other best buddy. They play school together and make up plays. They even have a best buddy theme song. But there are plenty of those other moments, too. Those moments when Zeke is pushing Julia's buttons. Those moments when she complains those commonly-proclaimed words of the first-born,

"I wish I was an only child!"

I had those moments too. And in those moments, I can tell Julia to appreciate Zeke until I am blue in the face. The fact of the matter is, occasionally, they will continue to annoy each other. One day, horror of horrors, Zeke may even want to date some of Julia's friends. But he will also be her biggest ally. And she will be his.

You see, perhaps the real problem with brothers is this: you rarely realize what a precious gift they are until you are grown.

70 Preserving Innocence

I was eight years old when I learned the words to Bow Wow
Wow's 80s hit, "I Want Candy." I was eight years old when
I learned that sometimes words have multiple meanings. It was our babysitter
who burst my bubble.

"I--- want candy! Bum, bum, bum, bum-bum. I--- want candy!"

The tune and rhythm were catchy and addictive. And as a charter
member of the Sugar Fan Club, I couldn't have agreed more with the lyrics!
As I bounced down the hallway on that Friday night singing the song, my
teenage babysitter gave me a serious look.

"Do you know what that song is about?" she asked.

"It's about candy!" I said. Duh. Where did my mom find this girl?

"No, it's not," she said in a tone more like a whisper.

"Well, what's it about then?" I probed. I leaned in. She leaned in.

"You should ask you parents," she began. "But, it has something to do
with the reason that men don't wear shirts to bed."

Huh?

"Will you just tell me what it's about?" I pressed.

She got very close and whispered in my ear, "No way!"

We spoke of it no more that evening, and of course, I did not ask my
parents. I was quite certain that they would not know. I did ask my dad why
he did not sleep with a shirt. He said he did sleep in a shirt. So that was that.

Although I was never told the reason the song was not appropriate
to sing, I never did hear it the same way again. I felt shame for singing it.

Now I knew that it was really not about jelly beans and licorice sticks. The innocence was gone.

We have had to fight the culture for several years now already. Back to school shopping gets harder every year, as Julia has begun to grow out of all the kid stores. Now we are faced with clothing options that include shirts with skulls on them, faux leather pants, and shorts with words written across the rear end. My daughter will never wear words like "hot stuff" or "heart-breaker" on her butt. Not while I am alive!

She has already been teased by kids at school for not being allowed to watch PG-13 movies. She is no stranger to the word, "inappropriate." But we are the gatekeepers to her innocent mind. So we must stay vigilant.

Julia really wanted to be in the talent show. It was going to be on the last day of her drama camp, and she had chosen a song that was very popular with the tweens. Although she does not listen to popular music on the radio, the song has been used on one particular TV channel that she frequently watches. The night before the talent show, she shared her selection with us. Michael and I knew right away that she did not know what she was singing about. One line included the phrase, "it feels like an overdose." There was no way on earth we were going to allow her to sing that in a talent show! Sweet thing didn't even know what an overdose was. Michael did a little more research and watched the video online. As he headed into her room, I knew that we were about to have drama and a very disappointed little girl.

"Sweet girl. I am really sorry to disappoint you," he began. "But your mother and I do not think this song is appropriate for you to sing at the talent show. You will need to choose something else."

"But it is tomorrow!" she argued. "I have already made up a dance to go with it. What's inappropriate about it?"

"We are not going to talk about it," Michael said. "But it is our job as your parents to protect your innocence for as long as we can. The world wants to trick you with its catchy tunes and rhythms and then take your innocence away. We are not going to let that happen."

As Michael frequently does, he chose just the right words. I wanted to applaud his speech. I also wanted to ask him why men don't sleep in shirts. But I did not.

After doing our parental duty, we both left the room and went about our separate activities. I could hear Julia crying in her room. So I made the trip back in. It was then that I had a brainstorm.

"Julia, do you remember the Britt Nicole album that I bought you a couple of years ago?" She nodded and wiped a tear away.

"You had the first song memorized. Do you think you still remember it?" I saw her spark return. "Yes! I think I do."

We listened to the song together. The words began to come back to her. We worked on a few moves that she could incorporate into her performance. We picked her outfit. And then we cuddled side by side on her pink bed and talked about it.

"You have a really great opportunity here," I told her. "You can use your singing talents to be a witness to others about your faith."

She liked that idea and hugged me tightly. "That's what I want to do, Mom."

I was so proud of her maturity. I didn't think I could be prouder. But the next day, I was.

Julia went first. She smiled at me from on stage. She put her hand on the microphone. And then she opened her mouth and sang:

> I wanna set the world on fire
> Until it's burning bright for You . . .
>
> Take my dreams, come and give them wings
> Lord with You, there's nothing I cannot do.
> ("Set the World on Fire"—Britt Nicole, Cindy Morgan, and
> Jason Ingram)

The camp teacher beside me leaned over and whispered, "I love those words!"

"I do, too," I said proudly. She would never know how close we came to "feels like an overdose."

I think Julia was a little surprised by the applause that she received when she finished the song. The audience really loved it. Particularly the moms! She was excited to share the experience with her daddy when he got home from work that night. We showed him the video from my phone and relived the applause one more time.

Julia and I discussed it more that night at bedtime.

"Mom, you know how the song talks about God using our dreams to make a difference? I think I know what I can do. You know how I love designing fashion? I could make a line of clothes for girls that look really good but still preserves their innocence!"

"What a fantastic idea!" I commended.

"Do you really think I can do it?" she asked.

"Totally!" I beamed.

"Now will you tell me what that other song is about?"

I hugged my little girl close and whispered in her ear.

"No way."

My babysitter would have been so proud.

> My hands, my feet, my everything;
> My life, my love, Lord, use me.
>
> I'm gonna set the world on fire.
> ("Set the World on Fire"—Britt Nicole, Cindy Morgan, and
> Jason Ingram)

71 Man's Best Friend

It was love at first sight for me. It was his deep, chocolate brown eyes that did it.

As I headed down my familiar route from work, I saw him on the side of the road beside the handwritten sign: "Puppies for Sale." He was no bigger than the length of my forearm, black and brown and white, the cutest thing I had ever seen. As Michael and I were early in the third year of our marriage, we were in the market for a "training baby." I knew in my heart this was that baby. My heart sank a little after the woman selling the puppies told me her asking price: Two hundred dollars. Pretty steep for a young couple just starting out in a new house. But, as she explained, he was purebred. His parents were both dog-show winners. He would come with Kennel Club papers and everything. As I looked into those deep, chocolate brown eyes for the first time, it was as if he were already mine. I asked the woman to hold him back for me, for just a little while.

"I need to talk to my husband," I explained. She understood and agreed to give me a few hours to make up my mind.

"You need to hurry," she cautioned. "This is my last male and he will go quickly."

Michael agreed, sight unseen, provided that I promised to haggle a little on the price. I went to the ATM and within a couple of hours, we had our first child. I proudly took my new baby to the pet store where I loaded up on all the supplies we would need: a water bowl, a food bowl, a big bag of puppy food and way too many toys.

We named him Zeus. His full name was Zeus Afreus Biggalo Simpson. Michael had come up with it. I had liked Snickers, but Michael convinced me that it was too generic a name. Zeus was a purely ironic name for such a small dog. Somehow, it just seemed right. After all, our miniature dachshund believed he was the god of thunder. We could tell it in his bark.

I developed a love/hate relationship with that bark. Although it did make me feel safer, it was also a nuisance. Zeus barked at everything that he perceived as a threat to our family. And that was just about everything. We invested in a shock collar. Michael even tried it on himself first to be sure it was not too powerful a shock. Zeus was persistent. We took off the collar. It was too hard to continue to punish him when he was only trying to protect us. The collar went into the trash. And Zeus moved into our bed.

We didn't have a big bed when we were newly married. That is the stage in marriage when you like bumping into each other throughout the night. Zeus made himself at home at our feet. Then, in between our feet. Then, in between my legs. But, being a cold-natured person, I saw this as a blessing for me in the winter time. Zeus was my own personal electric blanket.

We knew early on that our Zeus was gifted. Most people just teach their dog how to go potty outside. Our Zeus learned how to ring a bell hanging from the doorknob to signal us that he needed to go. Throughout the day, we would hear the little bell. And we would answer his need. It was a great system. And we were proud of our little boy.

A year passed by. Seasons changed. Big news came. A human baby was coming! For nearly three months we looked through name books, read parenting guides, dreamed about our November baby. Then the spotting started. The doctor confirmed our worst fears. We were losing the baby.

I had never struggled with depression before that time. But this loss was too much for my heart to bear. The doctor sent us home to wait for the inevitable. We pulled out the sofa bed, and that is where I stayed for five days. Michael and I watched movies to distract our minds. We watched TV and ate lots of cobbler. And all the time, Zeus comforted us. His deep, chocolate brown eyes told me all that he wanted to say. "It's going to be all right, Mommy" and "I am so sorry." He licked my tears. He listened to me cry and pray aloud as my faith went down this unjust and gut-wrenching road. All the while, he was there. He never, ever left my side.

Within another year and a half, Julia was born. My mom and dad were nervous about the way Zeus would react to this new, fragile person in the house. Michael and I knew in our hearts that Zeus would never harm her. This was confirmed on her first night in the nursery.

"Where is Zeus?" we asked each other, as we began to head in the direction of Julia's room.

And that is where we found him. Lying on the floor beside her crib. No barking. Just watching. He was protecting her. He lifted his head and looked at us for a minute as if to say, "Everything is good in here. I've got this."

This transition was not easy for Zeus though. One morning several months later, I found him lying on the floor beside the back door. He had been ringing the bell for minutes. We were so enthralled with Julia we hadn't even heard. After a while, he had given up the ringing and just decided to lie beside the door and wait. I took the bell down that day, as we surmised that it was posing a choking hazard to our new crawler, and we weren't hearing it anyway.

"Sorry, Zeus," I said casually, and let him out.

We would say that a million times through the next seven years, as Zeus was accidentally stepped on, kicked, or neglected. We loved him, but he took his place at the back of the line behind our human babies.

His first seizure was absolutely terrifying to us. We raced him to the emergency vet, who quickly hooked him up to an intravenous and began giving him medications and fluids. The bill came to four hundred dollars. He was diagnosed with epilepsy and we were given a prescription for phenobarbital which would supposedly stop the seizures. The medication made him sleepy and his eyes looked dull. And despite the medication being in his system, he continued to have seizures, although they only happened about once or twice a year. We decided to discontinue the medication. We wanted our old Zeus back.

Time went on and outside of the occasional seizure, Zeus was in fine shape. Well, for an overweight wiener dog, that is. We nicknamed him Chubbs. He went on trips with us. He went camping with us. He participated in every family holiday at my parents' house. He was fed table scraps, in addition to his weight-reduction dog food! His name was incorporated into the kids' prayer at night. He took his place in the prayer right after the grandmas and before the extended family.

The decision to move Zeus out of our bed came when we invested in a brand new bed. Having two, young children made sleep a luxury early on, and good sleep was a hot commodity. So, we put the cushion from one of our old chairs on the floor and built him a bed fit for a king. A prince, actually. Michael would frequently tell him in the evenings, "Good night, sweet prince." Spoiled much? I think so. He was getting older though, and having a bed on the floor was easier on his joints than having to jump up onto furniture. He had also developed cataracts in his eyes that made his aim a little off. We piled his bed with sheets, an old sleeping bag, and my Snuggie. He slept great there and we did too. Seasons came and went. Children began to grow up. And life went on as usual until August 28.

His longest seizure came on August 28. We had made the decision years ago that we would not be able to afford the four hundred dollar treatment plan each time a seizure came. However, as this one raged on for over three hours, we began to realize that something was very different and terribly wrong this time. I called the vet who suggested that we go to the emergency vet and then put him back on the phenobarbital. We would not know if there had been brain damage, but it was likely. The vet explained that Zeus's brain was learning how to have "better" seizures. It was likely that his next one would be even longer. As I reported this information and the vet's recommendation to Michael, both of our eyes filled with tears. It was clear what needed to be done.

After eleven years, it was time to say goodbye to our boy. Michael explained the situation to Julia. I talked to Zeke.

"Will Zeus be okay?" they both asked, as we were making arrangements for my parents to come and stay with the children.

"No," I replied. And even as I knew the answer I was giving, my own heart sank in saying it. "I think Zeus is going to go to heaven today."

The kids responded as we thought they would. Both in tears. Julia in full-on wailing mode; Zeke watching to see how others were reacting. We took a couple of pictures of Zeus in Michael's arms. The kids each gave Zeus a hug and a kiss and told him goodbye. Then we placed the children into Mom and Dad's loving arms and turned our attention to our first born "baby."

On the way to the animal hospital, Michael held Zeus tightly in a towel from home. It was a tradition that whenever Zeus was boarded during a long trip, we would leave him with a towel from home. He slept best under a blanket or a towel. We wanted him to smell his home. This trip was no different, although at the same time, it was heartbreakingly different. This would be his last time to smell home. Michael was sobbing and holding him closely. The seizure had stopped at this point and we had our old Zeus back. He was exhausted and was shaking.

"Zeus is a good boy," Michael repeated again and again. Zeus's little tail wagged a little bit upon hearing this familiar phrase of affirmation.

I could barely fill out the paperwork. The staff was very compassionate as they took us back to wait for the doctor. They took Zeus for a minute to put the catheter in place and then brought him back to us. I put the towel from home over the table cover that they had brought in. And we laid Zeus down on it.

We had a few moments to say what we needed to say. I told Zeus that I loved him and that I was sorry for all the times I was short with him or yelled at him for his barking. Michael told him thank you for all the years of protection that he had given to our family. We both thanked him for his compassion when we were sad, and for his companionship that we had taken for granted through the years. We told him he was a good dog and that we loved him so much. We told him that we were going to miss him.

And then, even though we were not really ready, we rang the bell for the doctor. There would be two shots, the doctor explained. The first shot was a sedative, and with it, his trembling stopped. His body relaxed into the towel that he rested on. It was a precious and intimate moment as Michael and I both got very close to his face and kissed him again and again. And then, with the second shot, those deep, chocolate brown eyes closed for the last time.

Michael says we will never get another dog. It would not be respectful. I don't know what the future will bring. But for now, we are talking a lot about heaven in our house. The kids like to think that Zeus is up there playing with

Little Granny, who always had a soft spot in her heart for him. I don't know if dogs go to heaven or how theologically sound that idea is, but sometimes, you have to put theology aside and just find comfort in what should be.

The house is much quieter now. I still miss him terribly. The back door has not opened much since that day, although if you look carefully, the door is still scarred from the bell of so many years ago. Zeus is still included in our family prayer at night. None of us are in a hurry to take his name out. He will always be a precious part of our family.

Man's best friend.

72 Generosity

My earliest memories of generosity were moments of disappointment. I remember charging into the back door after a long day at school, only to meet the delicious smell of a cake in the oven, or cookies cooling on the top of the kitchen counter.

"Mmmm," I would compliment. "Can I have some?"

Nine times out of ten, my mom would answer, "Sorry, honey. Those are for _____. I am taking them dinner tonight." They just had a baby . . . just had a funeral . . . just got married . . . just needed sugar.

Disappointment. See what I mean?

To be fair, my mom did bake for our family, too. In fact, my chubby tummy as a child was proof that I was not neglected in the area of treats. I had more than enough. But, it seemed a shame to waste such homemade goodness on whatever their names were. Why in the world were we doing that?

As I got older, there was more disappointment. I wanted a new stereo or jeans from the Gap. Instead, my dad wrote checks to missionaries. As embarrassing as it is to confess now, I can actually remember getting mad at my dad.

"Why are you sending *them* all of our money?" (It was not actually *all* our money. And it was not actually *my* money at all.)

"They are spreading the Gospel!" my dad (who has missionaries and preachers on his family tree like apples on an apple tree) would answer with great enthusiasm.

"Well, you could be helping *me*!" (I was not actually spreading the Gospel. At least, not intentionally.)

Disappointment.

I also remember well the day that it all changed. The day that generosity took on a sweeter, deeper meaning. It was Christmas time. The Porter family knew our family from church. She was a hard-working, single mom, raising five children alone. My parents were touched by her diligent efforts to be a good mother, when it would have been much easier just to yell out, "Every man for himself!" and run away to Mexico!

For some reason, my dad invited me to go with him to deliver the gift. As we drove up the dusty, dirt road that became their driveway, some of the kids came running to meet the car. They were smiling. They didn't know they were poor. I stayed in the car and looked out the window at the transaction that was taking place. It was a quick moment—the moment that my father's generosity blessed that family. But, watching from the car, my heart was changed. It made an impact on me forever. As he handed the woman the plain, white envelope, my heart was overflowing. But this time, it wasn't disappointment I was feeling. It was pure joy. She wiped tears from her cheek and hugged my dad and I could tell that she was already blessed, before she even opened the envelope. The children would have Christmas presents. They would have some good food. The kids might even get some new clothes or a new pair of shoes. Through that simple gift, lives were changed for the better.

Giving was way better than a new stereo or jeans from the Gap.

Michael and I will be the first to confess, we are not consistent in our church giving. But, we try to live generous lives. Some months, it means sending flowers to a friend who is hurting or sick. Some months, it means giving to a cause someone is fighting to support. Some months, it goes to a single mom at Michael's workplace, who just needs a little help. We support a little boy in Mississippi through a child-help organization. The kids pray for him every night. It is our prayer that Julia and Zeke will develop hearts that care for others too—that they will live in the truth that none of this world actually belongs to us anyway. It is all a gift from God. One day, we will leave all this stuff behind, even our stereos and jeans.

At age nine, Julia is starting to get it. The proof came at Christmas this year. As is my tradition, I had stocked up on Bath & Body Works lotions for all of the kids' teachers. Somehow, I had miscounted and bought one extra bottle of lotion. "If you can think of someone to give it to, you may have it," I told her. "If not, you can just keep it for yourself." I assumed that the second option would be the most attractive one. She disappeared into her room for what seemed like a long time. When she came out, she brought the lotion with her, wrapped up, with a note attached. What I saw brought tears to my eyes.

> *Thank you for the hard work that you do.*
> *I know you probably don't get thanked too much, but you should.*
> *Merry Christmas.*
>
> *Love, Julia*

"Who is this for?" I inquired.

"It is for Ms. Johnson."

Ms. Johnson is a special education aide at Julia's elementary school.

"She helps a girl who has a lot of problems and pushes her around in a wheelchair all day. I think it is probably really heavy to push, but she is always smiling. The other teachers will probably get a lot of presents, but I don't think she will. So I am giving her the lotion."

A tender heart. An insightful act. A blessing not only to Ms. Johnson's heart, but to my mommy heart as well.

Generosity.

"It is more blessed to give than to receive" (Acts 20:35).

The Big Picture

So we fix our eyes not on what is seen, but on what is unseen,
since what is seen is temporary, but what is unseen is eternal.

—2 CORINTHIANS 4:18

I still remember the moment I became a mother. As the doctor held my baby girl up over the paper curtain for me to see, my life was changed forever. I remember her first cry and her new baby smell. I remember the joy I felt as we buckled her into the car seat for the first time, and the yellow and black Onesie that we brought her home in. I remember the words to all of the lullabies that I sang to her and the noises that she made when she slept. And if I try really hard, I can still remember what her breath felt like on my neck as we shared many nights in the rocking chair together. But all of these memories, like the rest of life, will fade over time. It is already hard for me to remember her as a toddler. With the passing of each birthday, my relationship with her, and my picture of her, changes. Baby Julia has been replaced by big girl Julia, who is too quickly on her way to adolescent Julia.

In those early days of motherhood, when sleep deprivation is in full gear, it seems that the days and nights go on forever. Feeding, changing, playing, sleeping, again and again. Experienced mothers frequently share this truth with new mothers:

Treasure these days. They go so quickly.

I must have heard those statements fifty times after Julia was born. And then fifty more times after Zeke was born. I am sure that at the time I rolled my eyes and said, "I wish!" New mothers, struggling to "get it right" sometimes miss this truth. There is so much to be done: an unending stream of laundry, hours dedicated to feeding, and cleaning, and caring for the baby. And there is so much crying! (And sometimes the baby cries, too.) Even surrounded by baby-oriented tasks, it's easy to miss the moments. All the while, those precious days are passing.

Mary, the mother of Jesus, seemed to know this, even as a new mother. There she was, lying in the hay with her new baby boy, surrounded not by attentive nurses, air conditioning, and ice cream from the cafeteria, but by dirty, curious animals and dirty, curious shepherds. She must have been so overwhelmed in that moment. She was a newlywed, still getting used to being married. She was young. This was all new territory. What was to come? But the Bible does not paint a picture of a frazzled, insecure woman. It says this: "But Mary treasured up all these things and pondered them in her heart" (Luke 2:19).

This same sentiment is repeated later, after Mary and Joseph find their lost son in the temple. They had been back-tracking for days searching for him. We would expect her to respond with scolding, even with fearful anger perhaps. Yet, once again, even in that emotionally-charged moment, " His mother treasured all these things in her heart" (Luke 2:51).

I think Mary could see the big picture.

Can you?

How much time have we spent worrying about trivial things that do not matter? How much of our time is wasted on things that will not last? This is perfectly exemplified in the never-empty laundry basket. I am sure that you have one in your house too. As soon as the last load of clean clothes has been put away, someone is stripping off dirty ones to put back in the basket. There is not even time for an empty basket celebration! By the time you would get the invitations out to the party, some stinky gym sock would jump into the basket and ruin the festivities. The joy of an empty laundry hamper is short-lived.

The same thing could be said of all of our earthly tasks. All but one. The exception is our job as mothers. But how easily we can lose sight of that. How easily we can place our job as parents on an equal level with our laundry gig, or even on a lower level! How many times have I said, "I can't play right now, I am doing the laundry."

We have been entrusted with walking, talking miracles, made in the very image of our God. We hold in our arms a little piece of eternity. Everything on earth will pass away.

But the precious souls of our children will live on. This is a higher calling. It is an eternal one. Friends, no matter what stage you are in as a parent, let us agree not to lose sight of this.

Here are some ways to start:

- Fill their minds with spiritual truths about God. He is good. He is always with us, when we are happy and when we are sad. He can be trusted. He is faithful. He will make things right in the end.
- Pray for your children and with your children. Encourage them to pray about everything that is on their heart, even if it seems silly to you.
- Practice unconditional love and give grace, along with hugs and kisses, lavishly and often.
- Apologize when you are wrong. Then, ask for their forgiveness. It creates humility in you and demonstrates to them that they are people of value.
- Be joyful. Even in the midst of trials. Then explain to them where you find the strength.
- "I love you" cannot be said too many times in a day. Make sure love looks like something.
- And, from time to time, go and sit on your big kid's bed and watch them sleep, just for old time's sake.
- Treasure the moments that are given. After all, life's too short to miss the big picture.

About the Author

Melanie Fudge Simpson graduated from Abilene Christian University in 1995 with a bachelor of music degree. She taught elementary music in public schools for six years, during which time she was awarded the honor of Teacher of the Year in Katy Independent School District (Cimarron Elementary). In addition to teaching, Melanie has worn many professional hats: children's minister, worship leader, event coordinator, and choir director. Currently she teaches piano and voice through her business, Melanie's Melody. Her proudest role, however, is that of mother. She shares her adventures in motherhood on her popular online blog: *www.melaniesimpson.com*. In addition to writing, she enjoys singing, playing the piano, and running. She does not enjoy washing clothes or cleaning the bathroom, but she does those things anyway. Melanie lives in Katy, Texas with her handsome (and incredibly patient) husband of fourteen years, Michael, and their two angelic children, Julia and Zeke.